SQUIRES KITCHEN'S GUIDE TO

cake
shaping

Helen Penman

fun novelty cakes for all occasions

First published in March 2011 by
B. Dutton Publishing Limited, The Grange,
Hones Yard, Farnham, Surrey, GU9 8BB.
Copyright: Helen Penman 2011
ISBN-13: 978-1-905113-19-4
All rights reserved.
Reprinted in August 2011

Publisher: Beverley Dutton
Editor: Jenny Stewart
Art Director/Designer: Sarah Ryan
Deputy Editor: Jenny Royle
Designer: Zena Manicom
Sub Editor/Graphic Designer: Louise Pepé
PR and Advertising Manager: Natalie Bull
Photography: Alister Thorpe
Printed in China

Acknowledgements

Thanks to Dyck at Kit Box who provided cutters
and equipment for this book.

Thank you to Beverley, Jenny, Sarah and the team
at Squires. I never thought I would achieve this and
without their support over the years I wouldn't have
the ability and experience to write this book.

introduction

When I first started making cakes I was always a little worried
that my children wouldn't recognise the novelty cake I had
carved laboriously for their birthday! They always loved them
but the apprehension remains when receiving a call from a
customer wanting a carved novelty cake. Will they recognise
the creation? Will I ruin it by carving off too much? Fortunately
they have always worked out well!

So to take the worry out of carving cakes and to encourage
beginners to have a go, I have compiled this book as a guide,
introducing the basic shapes and creating easy novelty cakes
that will get you started, confident in the knowledge that the
cake will be fantastic!

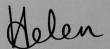

Dedication

I would like to dedicate this book to my long-suffering family – they have had to put up with ironing their own shirts for work or school and eating endless meals that have been thrown into the slow cooker!

contents

preparation

projects

equipment

for baking and carving

(1) **Dowelling rods:** these are either made of wood or food-grade plastic and provide internal support for cakes where needed. I use plastic dowels which can be sterilised with clear alcohol or boiling water before use. Insert them into the covered cake, mark level with the cake covering to the length you require, pull them out and lay flat on a cutting board. Using a craft knife, cut off the excess (if you cut through them part way, you can snap them off to the length required) and then re-insert into the cake.

(2) **Icing sugar shaker:** dust the work board and rolling pin lightly with icing sugar when rolling out to prevent the sugarpaste from sticking. A sugar shaker ensures that there are no lumps and controls the flow of icing sugar.

(3) **Measuring spoons:** I find these essential for accurately measuring ingredients for cakes.

(4) **Non-slip mat:** place under the work board to prevent it from moving as you work, and use in cake boxes and under the box when you are transporting cakes from one place to another.

(5) **Non-stick work board:** a large acrylic board is useful for rolling out large pieces of sugarpaste as it can be moved and cleaned easily.

(6) **Palette knives:** you will need a long, straight palette knife and a short, cranked palette knife. The long one is very useful for spreading large amounts of buttercream or jam onto layers of cake and to assist in the careful removal of any layers of cake. The smaller palette knife is useful when covering a carved cake to get the buttercream into smaller, more intricate spots.

(7) **Polythene food bags:** use these to keep sugarpaste fresh when not in use.

(8) **Ribbon:** always trim the edge of cake drums with 15mm width ribbon for a neat finish. Leave a slight overlap at the join and secure in place with either double-sided tape or a non-toxic glue stick.

(9) **Rolling pin, large:** a straight, acrylic pin is best as it gives a smooth finish to sugarpaste.

(10) **Rubber spatula:** I find this very useful for scraping cake mix or buttercream from bowls so there is no wastage.

(11) **Ruler and tape measure (not pictured):** use both to ensure cakes are the cut to the right size and height. The tape measure is extremely useful for measuring round curves of the cake where you need to ensure that the carving is accurate.

(12) **Scissors:** useful for cutting paste, ribbon and card for templates, keep a pair of fine scissors solely for sugarcraft use.

(13) **Sharp knives:** a large, serrated knife is needed for cutting layers in cakes and a smaller paring knife for trimming and shaping.

14 Smoothers: use either one or two to create a smooth, professional finish. I find the ones that have a flat edge very useful as this enables you to achieve a sharp right angle on the cake drum.

15 Spacers: use these when rolling out sugarpaste to ensure that it has an even thickness.

16 Spare cake drums: you will often need spare boards on which to carve and cover cakes and for temporarily holding cakes that will be stacked. You will also need one when using a spirit level (see below).

17 Spirit level: an important piece of equipment that is used to check that a cake is level. A simple DIY one is fine as long as it never gets used in the workshop! Always place a spare board or a sheet of greaseproof paper underneath it so it never comes into contact with the cake.

18 Turntable: this makes the covering and decoration of a cake much easier. I have a tall one that tilts the cake up as well as turning it, and another which is only a few centimetres deep, so the cake stays close to the level of the work surface.

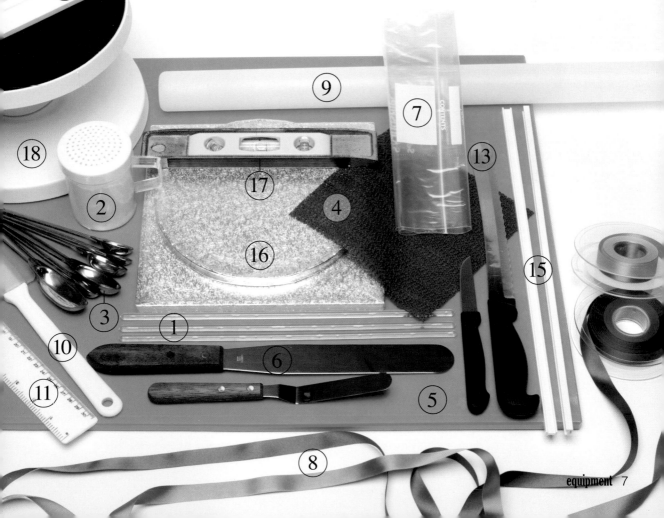

equipment

for cake decorating

1. **Bone tool:** the shape of this tool is perfect for indenting paste and for smoothing areas that are difficult to reach.

2. **Cocktail sticks:** use these for adding small amounts of concentrated food colour to sugarpaste.

3. **Craft knives:** it is useful to have two, one for cutting paste to give a sharp, accurate finish and another for cutting templates from paper.

4. **Cutters:** a huge range of cutters is available from sugarcraft suppliers, including flowers and leaves, geometric shapes and animals. Various cutters are used throughout the book – check the equipment list at the beginning of each project for specific requirements. Cutters are very useful if you are cutting out several shapes that must be identical, but if you don't have a specific cutter you can always make your own template from thin card and cut the shape with a craft knife or cutting wheel.

5. **Emery board or sandpaper (not pictured):** a new emery board or piece of fine sandpaper is very useful to sand small, fine pieces of dried flower paste before attaching to a cake. Sometimes even with the utmost care there are still some rough edges that need to be filed back to neaten them up. Keep for sugarcraft use only.

6. **Foam sponge:** food-grade sponge pieces are available from sugarcraft suppliers and are used to soften thin pieces of paste such as petals.

To thin, cup or frill a flower or petal, place it onto the foam and press firmly with a bone or ball tool.

7. **Forceps:** I use these for attaching very small, fine pieces where fingers can't reach.

8. **Kemper tool/mini palette knife:** a useful tool for picking up and trimming fine sugar pieces and applying buttercream to hard-to-reach places.

9. **Line marker:** ideal for marking a level line around the side of the cake to show where the cake should be sliced, or to mark a level line for easy piping.

10. **Non-stick board, small:** a small, acrylic board is useful for working on fine, detailed decorations for cakes (a green one will make it easy to see what you are working on).

11. **Paintbrushes and paint palette:** you will find it helpful to have a selection of brushes to hand including fine, pointed brushes for painting and gluing and large, flat brushes for dusting. Good quality brushes are available from sugarcraft suppliers (see page 92).

12. **Pencil, ruler (not pictured), rubber, tracing paper and card:** you will need all these for making templates. A cereal box is ideal for this purpose.

13. **Piping nozzles (tubes) and piping bags:** these are handy to have as they are used to decorate many of the cakes in this

15

17

book. The finer nozzles – 0 ,1 and 1.5 – are used to write inscriptions or to add fine details to cake work; larger nozzles are good for filling in areas with royal icing or other viscous liquids such as piping gel or SK Scintillo piping sparkles. You can make your own piping bags from greaseproof paper or you can buy them readymade. Plastic piping bags are also available, and you can choose from disposable and re-useable. These are particularly good with the larger nozzles that require larger quantities of filling, such as cream.

(14) **Posy pick:** this is inserted into the cake to hold wires or similar decorations that must not come directly in contact with the cake. Fill the pick with sugarpaste, then push in the wires so they are held securely. Finally, push the pick into the cake so that it is flush with the surface.

(15) **Ribbon cutter:** if you're making sugar ribbons, bands or strips this tool is very useful for cutting long, even strips of paste.

(16) **Rolling pin, small:** ideal for rolling out small amounts of flower paste, modelling paste, sugarpaste or marzipan.

(17) **Spare cake boards:** useful when you are making lots of small decorations that need to be kept to one side or for sliding the top slice of cake onto when filling a cake.

(18) **Stitching wheel (quilting tool):** this has a veining tool at one end and a wheel at the other that indents a stitched effect on paste.

(19) **Sugar shaper:** this versatile tool has different discs that can be inserted in the end to form softened sugarpaste or flower paste into different shapes and sizes for decoration. The single-hole 'string' disc is one of the most useful as well as the larger circle disc as this is the one that is used to make sugar sticks, i.e. short lengths of flower paste that are used for support in the cake so inedible supports don't have to be used.

(20) **Veining tool:** this has a multitude of uses, one of which is to accentuate lines in the paste to resemble creases.

edibles

Edible glue: this is needed to glue sugar items together. Brush a little glue onto the surface of the piece, then hold it in place and support with crumpled kitchen towel until the glue has dried. Edible glue can be bought readymade from Squires Kitchen or made using a small amount of white modelling paste mixed with boiled water. The homemade glue can be thinned down by adding more boiled water – always use boiled water to ensure there is no bacteria to cause it to go mouldy. A little gum arabic with cooled, boiled water is another good alternative to readymade edible glue.

Flower paste (gum paste): a paste that is normally used to make sugar flowers and leaves as it can be rolled very finely without tearing. In novelty work it is ideal for pieces that need to hold their shape as it dries quickly and very hard. It can also be added to sugarpaste to give it more stretch.

Food colourings: these are available as pastes, liquids and dusts. When colouring sugarpaste, flower paste, etc. I prefer to use paste colours rather than liquids because they don't change the consistency of the medium being coloured. Always add colour in small amounts using a cocktail stick – remember that you can add more but you can't

You can make your own sugarpaste, flower paste, marzipan and modelling paste if you wish. To save time I buy readymade sugarpaste which is available from sugarcraft shops and good supermarkets. The consistency of the paste does differ between brands, some are softer than others. I find a firmer sugarpaste is easier to work with but try various makes to see which suits you best.

take it out. Dust colours (powders) are applied to the surface of sugar pieces – they are excellent for adding a colour to a finished item to give shade and depth with a complementary colour or to add a contrasting colour to a small area. Ranges of dust colours are available with different effects such as metallic, glitter or lustre.

Mexican Modelling Paste (SK): a readymade paste that is ideal to use in moulds (as it is non-sticky), for modelling (as it holds its shape), and it can be folded, veined and creased with great results. Sometimes if a more supportive paste is needed, a little gum tragacanth can be added. The paste does need some support while drying but once dry it stays firm whilst remaining soft enough to cut and eat.

Royal icing: this is often used to stick decorations in place and to pipe details or inscriptions onto cakes. You can either make your own (see recipe on page 18) or use Squires Kitchen's Instant Mix Royal Icing where you just need to add water.

Sugarpaste (rolled fondant): usually used for the outer covering on novelty cakes as it is soft and

pliable, can be folded, indented and creased, and it can also be smoothed flat. I generally use white sugarpaste and colour it with paste colours, except where a very strong colour such as black is used – I always buy this ready coloured as it can get quite messy otherwise!

Sugar syrup: brush this onto baked Madeira sponge cake to ensure that it is moist and delicious. You can make your own with sugar and boiling water (see recipe on page 18) or buy flavoured syrup from supermarkets.

Vodka (or any colourless spirit): this is used to thin out paste colours for painting or to make paint from dusting powders. It leaves no taste and evaporates rapidly so the colours won't run when dry.

White vegetable fat: a little of this on your hands will help to soften up flower paste if it has dried out and can also be used to stop paste from sticking to the board and rolling pin instead of icing sugar. You will need to add a little white vegetable fat to paste when used with a sugar shaper to make it easier to extrude.

baking cakes

hints and tips

Whether you bake regularly or only on special occasions, here are a few tips that will help you achieve a perfect cake every time.

Follow the ingredient measurements carefully and stick to either metric or imperial throughout.

Allow your oven to get up to temperature before you put your cake in to make sure it bakes evenly.

Always line your cake tins with greaseproof paper: full instructions are given opposite.

Creaming butter and sugar requires vigorous beating to aerate the mixture, making it soft and fluffy. This can be done by hand but is quicker in a food mixer or processor if you have one. It is also much easier to achieve if the butter is soft: if you forget to get it out of the fridge, give it a blast in the microwave for 10 seconds.

I find that butter is much better than margarine as it has a finer flavour and, unlike oil, it can be beaten to incorporate air. Unsalted is best for cakes, although shortbread is heavenly when made with salted butter. Oil does have its place in cake making but this is usually when fruit is to be added into the mix to add moisture. Vegetable oil does have a lower saturated fat content than butter (which is an animal fat).

If the cake is frozen, take it out of the freezer at least 4 hours before you start working on it to allow it to thaw slightly.

Always use eggs at room temperature. Add the beaten eggs slowly and beat thoroughly between additions. This gives the mixture a much paler colour, keeps the texture light and will ensure the mixture doesn't curdle. If it does, sift a tablespoon of flour into the mixture and fold it in with a figure of '8' motion using a metal spoon. The metal spoon will slice the mixture without pulling it and removing all the air you have already got into the cake mix. Once the flour is mixed in, continue to add the egg.

Always use the best ingredients you can.

Don't be tempted to keep opening the oven to look at the cake; leave it until around 10 minutes before the full time is up and have a quick look, not opening the oven fully. If the centre is still uncooked the cold air will make it sink. If you find that you are regularly getting sunken cakes, try adding a little more flour to the mix to make it a little stiffer, but bear in mind this can make the cake dryer.

To test if the cake is baked, press the top with your fingers when you take it out of the oven. If it feels spongy and springs back it is ready. If you are still not sure, insert a skewer in the deepest part: it should draw back cleanly when the cake is cooked. Leave it in its tin until cold, then pack and store.

Before filling the cake, I always slice it in half and brush syrup over the two exposed sponge surfaces. I usually use vanilla but you can add other flavours such as toffee or cherry (see the recipe for cherry syrup in the black forest cake recipe, page 17). This is an excellent way of keeping the cake moist and accentuating the flavour.

Cakes are always easier to carve if they have been frozen first, they are much less crumbly. If you prefer not to freeze the cake completely, wrap it in greaseproof paper then foil and secure with tape. Place in the fridge for at least 24 hours before carving.

how to line a cake tin

You can buy many specialist tins in various shapes, but I find they are not really necessary unless you are going to use them frequently. It is excellent value to buy the multi-size square tin with adjustable internal walls that can be positioned to make numerous rectangles and squares in different sizes (available from sugarcraft suppliers, see page 92). Mini cakes are now very popular so if you are making these you can buy mini cake pans in different shapes and sizes; these reduce the time involved in making mini cakes and ensure they all come out exactly the same size, something that would be very time consuming if you were cutting out the shapes by hand. Do bear in mind that once you make mini cakes, you also have to cover them individually so make sure you leave yourself enough time!

Before baking a cake the tin should always be lined with greaseproof paper to prevent the cake from sticking to the tin. The lining should be done neatly so that when the mixture is added it isn't distorted by the lining.

You will need:

Cake tin

Pencil

Greaseproof paper

Scissors

Butter

Pastry brush

1   Use a pencil to draw around the outside base of the tin on a sheet of greaseproof paper.

2   Cut out the shape a little inside the line to fit the base of the tin.

3   Cut a strip of greaseproof paper to fit around the sides of the tin with an overlap at the join. The strip should be approximately 2.5cm (1") deeper than the tin. It doesn't have to be in one whole piece but must overlap if in pieces.

4   Fold the strip along one long edge of the paper, approximately 1.3cm (½") from the edge. Unfold then snip along this side at regular intervals to make a fringe.

5   Melt some butter and, using a pastry brush, grease the side of the tin.

6   Insert the lining so the fringed edge lies on the base of the tin.

7   Grease the base of the tin and insert the base lining so it lies on top of the fringe, making a neat edge around the base of the tin.

8   Grease the lining with melted butter.

If you decide to use a spherical tin rather than carve the cake yourself, follow these instructions for lining the tin.

1   Cut out a circle of greaseproof paper that is 10cm (4") larger in diameter than the tin. Fold the circle in half twice to mark the centre point.

2   Cut from the outer edge towards the centre of the circle: stop approximately 2.5cm (1") from the centre so that you don't just cut the paper into pieces. Continue all the way round the circle to make segments that are joined together at the centre.

3   Grease the inside of the tin with melted butter. Place the centre of the liner in the centre of the tin then arrange the segments, overlapping them as you work around the tin. Use more melted butter to secure them in place.

4   Repeat to line the other half-sphere.

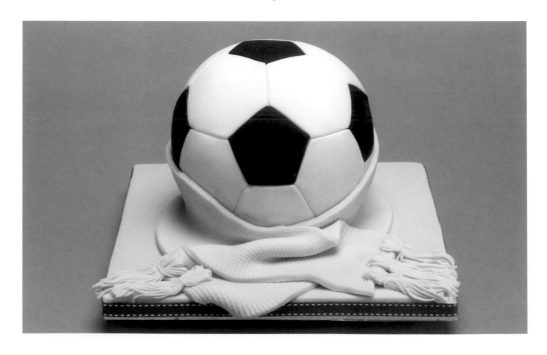

cake and icing recipes

Vanilla sponge							
Square	12.5cm (5")	15cm (6")	17.5cm (7")	20.5cm (8")	23cm (9")	25.5cm (10")	28cm (11")
Round	15cm (6")	17.5cm (7")	20.5cm (8")	23cm (9")	25.5cm (10")	28cm (11")	30.5cm (12")
Softened butter	175g (6oz)	260g (9oz)	430g (15oz)	510g (1lb 2oz)	690g (1lb 8oz)	770g (1lb 11oz)	940g (2lb 1oz)
Caster sugar	175g (6oz)	260g (9oz)	430g (15oz)	510g (1lb 2oz)	690g (1lb 8oz)	770g (1lb 11oz)	940g (2lb 1oz)
Eggs (medium)	3	4	7	8	10	11	13
Self raising flour	225g (8oz)	340g (12oz)	560g (1lb 4oz)	700g (1lb 8oz)	1kg (2lb 3oz)	1.14kg (2lb 8oz)	1.3kg (2lb 14oz)
Vanilla essence	½tsp	1tsp	2½tsp	3tsp	4tsp	4½tsp	5½tsp
Baking times	¾-1 hour	1-1 hour 10 minutes	1¼-1 hour 20 minutes	1½-1 hour 40 minutes	1¾-2 hours	2¼-2½ hours	2½-2¾ hours

1 Beat the butter and sugar together until fluffy and light in colour.

2 Beat the eggs, then add them to the mixture a little at a time, beating in thoroughly before adding more. If the mixture looks like it is splitting, add in a tablespoon of the flour.

3 Fold in the flour using a metal spoon.

4 Add the vanilla essence.

5 Transfer the mixture to the prepared baking tin, making sure that it is slightly lower in the centre.

6 Bake in a preheated oven at 180°C/350°F/gas mark 4, until the cake is a golden brown colour and springy to the touch.

Variation: lemon cake

• Substitute the vanilla in the recipe for concentrated lemon juice.

• When making the buttercream, add 10-20ml (½-¾fl oz) of lemon juice.

Variation: simple chocolate cake

• Add 25g (1oz) of cocoa for every 225g (8oz) of flour and 15ml (1tbsp) of milk for each 25g (1oz) of cocoa to ensure that the mixture is not too dry.

Chocolate sponge								
Square	12.5cm (5")	15cm (6")	17.5cm (7")	20.5cm (8")	23cm (9")	25.5cm (10")	28cm (11")	30.5cm (12")
Round	15cm (6")	17.5cm (7")	20.5cm (8")	23cm (9")	25.5cm (10")	28cm (11")	30.5cm (12")	33cm (13")
Softened butter	85g (2¾oz)	115g (4oz)	150g (5¼oz)	225g (8oz)	310g (10¾oz)	340g (12oz)	425g (14¾oz)	510g (1lb 2oz)
Soft brown sugar	195g (6¾oz)	285g (10oz)	450g (1lb)	560g (1lb 4oz)	720g (1lb 10oz)	860g (1lb 14oz)	1kg (2lb 3oz)	1.25kg (2lb 12oz)
Cocoa powder	20g (¾oz)	30g (1oz)	50g (1¾oz)	60g (2oz)	80g (2½oz)	90g (3oz)	110g (3¾oz)	120g (4¼oz)
Water	60ml (2fl oz)	90ml (3fl oz)	145ml (5fl oz)	175ml (6fl oz)	225ml (8fl oz)	260ml (9fl oz)	315ml (11fl oz)	370ml (13fl oz)
Plain flour	150g (5¼oz)	225g (8oz)	375g (13¼oz)	450g (1lb)	750g (1lb 10oz)	800g (1lb 12oz)	1.1kg (2lb 6oz)	1.35kg (3lb)
Baking powder	1¼tsp	2tsp	2½tsp	4tsp	4tsp	6tsp	7¼tsp	8½tsp
Bicarbonate of soda + salt	⅓tsp	½tsp	1¼tsp	2tsp	3tsp	3¾tsp	4tsp	4¼tsp
Vanilla essence	1tsp	1tsp	1¼tsp	2tsp	3tsp	3¾tsp	4tsp	4¼tsp
Eggs (large)	2	2	3	4	5	6	7	8
Sour cream	75ml (2½fl oz)	150ml (5fl oz)	200ml (7fl oz)	300ml (10½fl oz)	335ml (11¾fl oz)	450ml (15½fl oz)	540ml (19½fl oz)	580ml (1pt)
Baking times	¾-1 hour	1-1 hour 10 minutes	1¼-1 hour 20 minutes	1½-1 hours 40 minutes	1¾-2 hours	2¼-2½ hours	2½-2¾ hours	2¾-3 hours

1 Sift all the dry ingredients into a bowl.

2 Beat the butter and sugar together until light and fluffy in texture.

3 Beat the eggs and add to the butter mixture a little at a time. If the mixture looks like it is going to split, add a tablespoon of the dry ingredients, then continue adding the egg.

4 Add the vanilla essence and beat well. Add the sour cream and mix gently.

5 Fold the dry ingredients into the mixture using a metal spoon. Only add the water if the mixture is too stiff.

6 Carefully spoon the mixture into the prepared cake tin and bake in the centre of the oven for the suggested time at 190°C/370°F/gas mark 5.

Variation: chocolate and cherry cake

• Add 90g (3oz) of dried or glacé cherries to the basic recipe.

Variation: chocolate caramel cake

Make the caramel first to allow it to cool before adding it to the baked cake.

You will need:

225g (8oz) sugar

50g (2oz) butter

140ml (5fl oz) double cream

1   First, make sure you have all the ingredients weighed out and ready to use. Making caramel is a fast process so you will need to have everything to hand.

2   Heat the sugar on moderately high heat in a large, heavy-bottomed saucepan. As the sugar begins to melt, stir vigorously with a whisk or wooden spoon. When the sugar starts to boil, stop stirring.

3   As soon as all of the sugar has melted (the liquid sugar should be dark amber in colour), immediately add the butter to the pan. Whisk until the butter has melted.

4   Take the pan off the heat, slowly add the cream to the pan and continue to whisk. When you add the butter and the cream, the mixture will foam up considerably so make sure you use a large saucepan.

5   Whisk until the sauce is smooth. Allow the sauce to stand for a few minutes, then pour into a glass jar or jug and allow to cool to room temperature.

•   Make the chocolate cake following the basic recipe and allow to cool. Cut the cake in half horizontally then drizzle the caramel over the cut cakes and allow it to soak in. Don't add too much caramel otherwise the cake will be too soggy.

•   Add more of the caramel to the buttercream.

Variation: black forest chocolate cake

•   Add 45ml (3tbsp) of cherry brandy to the cake for every 225g (8oz) of flour. For a non-alcoholic version, use 225g (8oz) of morello cherries with 225g (8oz) of sugar and 100ml (3½fl oz) of water. Boil the ingredients together until the cherries are soft, mash with a potato masher and sieve to remove the skins and other fleshy bits.

•   Add 400g (14oz) of tinned cherries in syrup for every 250g (8¾oz) of flour. Roughly chop the cherries and save the syrup or make the syrup as above if using fresh cherries.

•   Add the cherry syrup to the buttercream filling.

Buttercream

The quantity of buttercream required is given at the beginning of each project so scale the ingredients up or down as needed. This recipe makes approximately 1.2kg (2lb 11oz) of icing, or enough to fill and cover a 28cm (11") round cake.

You will need:

225g (8oz) butter, softened

1kg (2lb 3¼oz) icing sugar

15-30ml (1-2tbsp) syrup (vanilla or a flavour of your choice to complement the cake) or fresh fruit juice

1 Beat the butter and add the icing sugar in small amounts until it is all incorporated and the mixture is smooth.

2 Add the syrup/flavouring a little at a time until the buttercream has a soft consistency; add more if a softer texture is needed (you might find this when crumb-coating the surface of cakes as a softer icing won't pull the cake into crumbs).

Sugar syrup

I use this for sprinkling over the cut slices of cake to add extra moisture and flavour.

You will need:

250ml (8¾fl oz) water

250g (8¾oz) caster sugar

1 Combine both ingredients in a saucepan, heat to dissolve the sugar and bring to the boil. Continue boiling until the volume has reduced by a quarter.

2 Allow to cool before use. The syrup can be stored in a sterilised jar in the fridge for up to 1 month.

Ganache

If you would like to fill the chocolate cake with a deliciously rich chocolate filling, ganache is the perfect choice! Follow the buttercream quantities given at the beginning of the projects as a guide; this recipe is enough to fill and cover a 23cm (9") cake. To save time you can buy it readymade from Squires Kitchen (see suppliers on page 92).

You will need:

500g (1lb 1½oz) dark chocolate, chopped

250ml (8¾oz) double cream

125g (4½oz) unsalted butter

1 Place the chopped, dark chocolate into a heatproof bowl.

2 Heat the cream and butter in a high-sided saucepan until it just starts to boil. Pour this over the chocolate and stir until smooth.

3 Leave the ganache to cool and harden then store in the fridge until required. If it is too stiff to spread, gently warm it in a double boiler (*bain marie*) to bring it to spreading consistency.

Royal icing

You will need:

2 egg whites from British Lion-marked eggs (or SK Fortified Albumen if you prefer not to use fresh eggs)

455g (1lb) icing sugar, sieved

1 Place the egg whites in a bowl and sieve the icing sugar over the top. Mix in thoroughly.

2 Keep adding icing sugar until the required consistency is achieved. For most applications in this book, the icing needs to be a little stiffer than runny; if it is too stiff, it will not act as a 'glue' to stick decorations in place.

recipes using cake crumbs

If you have any cake crumbs or trimmings left over after you have carved your cake there is no need to waste them. Some could be used as treats for your family (if the slices are big enough): just stick them together with buttercream. Some could be used in a trifle or are delicious heated up in the microwave with cream or custard. Alternatively, try one of these recipes to make the most of your cake!

If you don't have time to do anything with the cake crumbs when they're fresh, seal in small quantities in plastic food bags and freeze until you have more time. You should only do this if the cake has not already been frozen and thawed (see page 12).

Some of the recipes have alcohol in them so make a nice treat for the adults while the children are enjoying the celebration cake!

Refrigerator cake

You will need:

350g (12¼oz) dark chocolate

125g (4½oz) butter

35ml (2tbsp) golden syrup

450g (1lb) cake crumbs (whizz them in a food processor if the crumbs are not fine enough)

75ml (4tbsp) rum (or amaretto if you are using amaretto biscuits) or chocolate syrup for a non-alcoholic version

225g (8oz) crushed digestive biscuits (or amaretto biscuits)

50g (1¾oz) glacé cherries, roughly chopped

50g (1¾oz) sultanas (optional)

20.5cm (8") square cake tin, lined with greaseproof paper (bring the paper over the sides of the tin to make it easier to lift out the cake when set)

1 If you are using sultanas in the recipe, soak them in the rum/amaretto/chocolate syrup for 1 hour before making the cake.

2 Melt the chocolate, butter and golden syrup in a non-stick pan or in a microwave.

3 Add the cake crumbs and crushed biscuits. Stir thoroughly.

4 Add the glacé cherries and soaked sultanas if you are using them; if not, add the rum/amaretto/syrup at this stage too. Mix well.

5 Pour into the prepared tin and refrigerate for 1-2 hours until set.

6 Slice into 18 finger-sized slices.

Truffles

You will need:

125g (4½oz) dark chocolate

50g (1¾oz) unsalted butter

125g (4½oz) cake crumbs

50g (1¾oz) icing sugar

25ml (1tbsp) dark rum, brandy, or liqueur of your choice, or chocolate syrup for a non-alcoholic version

Chopped nuts, chocolate vermicelli, or cocoa powder (for coating)

1 Melt the chocolate and butter in a non-stick pan or in a microwave.

2 Add the cake crumbs, icing sugar and liqueur and mix well.

3 Place in the fridge for half an hour or so until the mixture starts to firm up.

4 Take about a teaspoon of mixture, shape into a ball and roll in the coating of your choice.

5 Leave to cool thoroughly in the fridge.

These work really well as gifts – place in little petit fours cases and present in a gift box. Alternatively, make cake pops by inserting a lolly stick and dipping into melted chocolate. Decorate with vermicelli or sugar sprinkles.

Bakewell tart topping

You will need:

50g (1¾oz) butter (softened)

50g (1¾oz) sugar

1 egg

50g (1¾oz) ground almonds

Almond essence

50g (1¾oz) cake crumbs

1 Beat the sugar and butter together until they are light and fluffy.

2 Add the egg and beat.

3 Add the ground almonds, almond essence and cake crumbs and mix well.

This makes a delicious topping for a Bakewell tart, giving it a more substantial texture than the traditional sponge topping.

top tip

You can always use up your cake crumbs in any recipe that asks for a biscuit base such as cheesecake or tart au chocolat – simply replace the biscuits in the recipe with cake crumbs.

portion chart

It is not always easy to work out how many portions you will get from a carved cake as they have been altered from their original shape. This chart gives an estimate for the number of slices you will get from each cake size, cutting the cake into rectangular shapes rather than wedges. Bear in mind that this is only a guideline: if you're unsure whether you will have enough cake, you can make it larger (remember to increase the amount of sugarpaste too) or bake cupcakes to match the main cake.

Size	Round	Square
12.5cm (5")	7	8
15cm (6")	11	14
17.5cm (7")	15	20
20.5cm (8")	20	27
23cm (9")	27	35
25.5cm (10")	34	45
28cm (11")	43	56
30.5cm (12")	50	67

preparing a cake

Trimming

For the most part, carved novelty cakes do not need to be trimmed (the brown crust removed from the outside of the cake) because as you cut your novelty cake to shape, you will most likely remove this anyway. If you have any left showing when you have finished, you can decide if it needs to be removed. As long as the crust isn't burnt I don't usually trim it off as it tastes as delicious as the rest of the cake.

Levelling

No matter how carefully you level the cake mixture before cooking, you will almost certainly find that it will rise and leave a domed top when baked. If the top isn't too raised or crispy you could leave it, turn it upside down so you have the flat base as the top of the cake and fill the gap around the bottom of the cake with small sausages of sugarpaste. This is particularly useful if your cake is rather shallow in depth as trimming the top flat would make it even shallower. Try to aim for around 7.5cm (3") as a depth for your cakes. If you find that they are consistently shallow in the tin despite following the correct amount of mix, make more mix to ensure that the tin is approximately ¾ full before baking. (Recommended quantities are given on pages 15 to 16.)

You will need:

Side marker (Kit Box)

Ruler

Long, serrated knife

Palette knife

Spare cake drum or board

Small spirit level

1   To trim the top of a cake to a constant depth, use a side marker. Measure the lowest depth of the cake with the ruler, set the side marker to this depth, then scribe a line all the way round the top of cake as a cutting guide.

2 Follow the scribed line with the long, serrated knife, cutting carefully towards the centre of the cake. If you work your way around the cake, not going too deeply, you will find it easier to keep the cutting level. Remove the top crust and turn the cake over so you now have the bottom of the cake at the top.

3 Place a spare cake drum or board on top of the cake with the spirit level on top. Check that the cake is completely level.

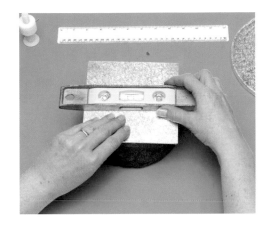

Cutting and filling

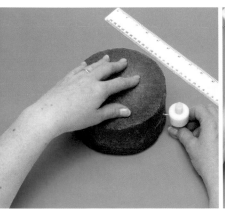

1 Measure the cake again and set the side marker to scribe a line all the way round the centre of the cake. If the cake is deep, set the marker at 2-3cm (approximately 1") intervals.

2 Using the long, serrated knife, cut into the centre of the cake along the scribed line as before.

3 Remove the top layer of cake by sliding it onto a spare cake drum. This is the easiest way to remove the cake without it breaking into pieces.

4 Fill the cake with buttercream using the palette knife, then replace the top section of cake by sliding it carefully from the drum back onto the cake.

guide to using templates

All of the templates required for the projects in this book are supplied at the back (see pages 88 to 91). There are instructions for enlarging them to the correct size, although you can make them bigger or smaller to suit the number of guests.

You will need:

Greaseproof/tracing paper

Pencil

Thin card or an empty cereal packet

Sharp scissors or a craft knife and cutting board

Glass-headed pins, sterilized

Small, sharp knife

1   Enlarge the template to the size required using a photocopier or scanner.

2   Trace the shape onto greaseproof or tracing paper and cut out. If you are making a basic shape, use this as your template. For more elaborate shapes, trace the shape onto thin card and cut out.

3   Pin the template to the cake using glass-headed pins that have been sterilized with alcohol or boiling water.

Always use glass-headed pins because they are easier to see. Count the pins out as you use them and make sure you put them all away safely afterwards.

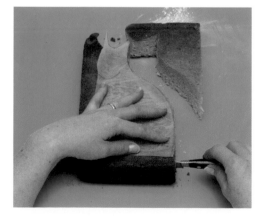

4   Following the template, carefully carve the cake using a small, sharp knife.

5   Remove the template and put the pins away safely. Use the knife to round off the edges of the cake.

6   Continue to create the shape required, following the step photographs as a guide.

covering a cake

Following these steps to cover your cakes will ensure that your cake has a professional appearance and gives you the perfect surface on which to complete your design.

You will need:

Cake and filling

Large, serrated knife

Spare cake drum

Palette knife or spatula

Sugarpaste (see each project for the quantity required)

Paste food colours (SK)

Large rolling pin

2 cake smoothers

Small, cranked palette knife

Spacers

Cocktail stick

Icing sugar in shaker

1   Prepare the cake by trimming, levelling, cutting and filling with your chosen flavour of buttercream (see pages 22 to 23). If the cake is deep (such as the spider), slice the cake every 2-3cm (approximately 1") so there is plenty of filling through the cake. Cut to shape following the instructions for your chosen project.

2   Using a palette knife or spatula, cover the outside of the sponge cake with a thin layer buttercream: this will help the sugarpaste stick to the cake and will keep any crumbs stuck to the cake and not in the sugarpaste. This is known as the crumb coating. Always prepare the cake to this stage before rolling

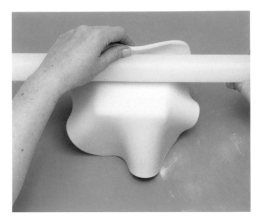

out the sugarpaste, otherwise the paste will start to dry and crack when covering the cake.

3 Colour the sugarpaste with paste colouring if required and roll out on a surface dusted lightly with icing sugar. Roll out using a large rolling pin, using spacers if you wish to ensure the paste is the same thickness throughout.

4 Check that the paste is the correct size by roughly measuring the top and sides of the cake with the rolling pin. The paste should be approximately 3-4mm ($^1/_8$") thick. Gently roll the paste over the rolling pin and transfer it to the cake. Carefully unroll the sugarpaste over the cake, making sure there is enough hanging over the cake sides to cover the cake completely.

5 Smooth the top of the cake gently with the palms of your hands, making sure there are no pockets of trapped air under the surface. Continue smoothing gently over the edge, allowing the paste to adhere to the cake, and continue smoothing the paste carefully down the sides of the cake.

6 Allow the excess paste to flatten out onto the cake drum and then use a sharp knife to trim it off, leaving about 5mm (just over $^1/_8$") still flat on the board.

7 Smooth the sides of the cake further and flatten the excess paste on the cake drum. Trim all the excess off to make a neat edge around the base.

8 Using two smoothers with the sharp corner edges at the bottom, smooth the sides of the cake evenly, paying particular attention to the trimmed edge of the paste. Gently smooth the top of the cake with the smoothers.

9 Make a pad of the same colour sugarpaste and flatten on the work surface to make sure the pad is smooth and free from cracks and lumps. Lightly 'polish' the cake with the pad, removing any grains of icing sugar and leaving a shiny, smooth surface. Pay particular attention to the curve of the paste over the top edge to smooth out any fine cracks in the paste.

covering a cake drum

Cake drums are 15mm thick, foil-covered cake boards that are used under the base of cakes. They come in all sorts of shapes and sizes, including round, square, oval and petal. All of the cakes in this book are presented on cake drums covered with sugarpaste and trimmed with co-ordinating ribbon.

There are two ways to cover a cake drum, one with the cake in position on the drum and the other before the covered cake is put in place. I usually find it easiest to cover the whole drum before placing the cake; the only exception is when the cake is a large size, making it difficult to lift onto the drum without damaging the cake covering. In this case it is easier to cover the cake first, then the cake drum.

You will need:

Cake drum (see each project for the shape and size required)

Kitchen roll

Cooled, boiled water

Sugarpaste

Icing sugar shaker

Large rolling pin

Sugarpaste

Smoother

Spacers (optional)

Sharp knife

Pizza wheel

Small turntable (optional)

Method 1: covering the whole drum

1   Lightly dampen the cake drum using kitchen roll dampened with cooled, boiled water, just enough to allow the sugarpaste to stick.

2   Lightly dust the work surface with icing sugar, then roll out the paste using a large rolling pin. You can use spacers to keep the thickness of paste even.

3   Roll out the paste into the general shape of the cake drum to be covered, until it is slightly larger than the cake drum. It should be approximately 5mm ($^1/_8$") thick.

4   Lift the paste onto the cake drum, using the rolling pin to help move the paste without stretching or tearing it.

5   Using the cake smoother, smooth the paste on the cake drum.

6   Cut around the edge of the drum with a sharp knife to remove the excess paste. Hold the knife against the edge of the drum as you cut to keep the edge straight.

7   Form a pad with the paste trimmings and smooth the cut edge, taking care not to tear it.

Method 2: covering the drum with the cake in position

1   Position the cake on the cake drum.

2   Roll out the sugarpaste on a work surface dusted with icing sugar to prevent sticking. This time, form a long sausage shape and keep the elongated shape as you roll it out.

3   Measure around the cake, then check the paste to see if it is long enough to go all the way around the drum. Dampen the drum using the kitchen roll.

4   Place the cake drum onto a small turntable if you have one (it makes it much easier to cover the drum if the cake will turn easily as you work).

5   Using the pizza wheel, trim along one long side of the paste to make a neat edge: this will be the edge that will go up against the covered cake. Slide a large palette knife under the paste to loosen it from the board.

6   Gently lift the paste a little at a time and position it up against the cake, working carefully so you don't tear the paste.

7   When you get all the way round, trim the two ends at the join, then smooth gently with a pad of paste. Smooth over the rest of the drum with the pad of paste.

8   Use the sharp knife to remove the excess paste and use the pad of paste again to smooth any rough edges.

cake covering quantities

All the cake sizes for the projects in this book are given at the beginning, but if you would like to make them bigger or smaller to suit the number of recipients, you can use this chart as a guide to the amount of cake filling and covering that you will need.

Cake size	Buttercream/ganache	Sugarpaste covering	Sugarpaste for drum
10cm (4")	150g (5¼oz)	500g (1lb 1½oz)	100g (3½oz)
12.5cm (5")	225g (8oz)	600g (1lb 5¼oz)	150g (5¼oz)
15cm (6")	300g (10½oz)	700g (1lb 8¾oz)	200g (7¼oz)
18cm (7")	450g (1lb)	750g (1lb 10½oz)	250g (8¾oz)
20.5cm (8")	600g (1lb 5¼oz)	1.25kg (2lb 12¼oz)	300g (10½oz)
23cm (9")	750g (1lb 10½oz)	1.5kg (3lb 5oz)	325g (11½oz)
25.5cm (10")	1kg (2lb 3¼oz)	2kg (4lb 6½oz)	400g (14¼oz)
28cm (11")	1.25kg (2lb 12¼oz)	2.2kg (4lb 13½oz)	475g (1lb ¾oz)
30.5cm (12")	1.5kg (3lb 5oz)	2.4kg (5lb 4½oz)	500g (1lb 1½oz)
33cm (13")	1.75kg (3lb 13¾oz)	2.75kg (6lb 1oz)	550g (1lb 3½oz)
35.5cm (14")	2kg (4lb 6½oz)	3kg (6lb 9¾oz)	575g (1lb 4¼oz)

PROJECTS

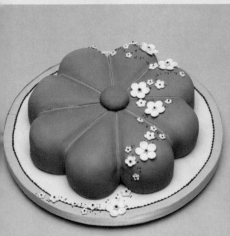

number 6 friendly fish

edibles

25.5cm x 20.5cm (10" x 8") rectangular sponge cake

225g (8oz) buttercream

Sugarpaste: 2.5kg (5lb 8¼oz) white

SK Mexican Modelling Paste (MMP): 350g (12½oz) White

SK Sugar Florist Paste (SFP): 20g (¾oz) Black

SK Professional Designer Paste Food Colours: Desert Storm, Sunny Lime, Yucca

SK Double Strength Professional Paste Food Colours: Hyacinth, Hydrangea

Small amount royal icing

equipment

2 x 30.5cm x 25.5cm (12" x 10") rectangular cake drums

'6' template (see page 88)

In addition to the edibles and equipment listed here, you will also need some basics before starting the project:

Edibles, see pages 10 to 11.

Equipment for Baking and Carving, see pages 6 to 7.

Equipment for Cake Decorating, see pages 8 to 9.

1 Colour 200g of sugarpaste with Hydrangea Paste Food Colour to make a deep turquoise, 200g of white paste to a soft grey by adding 10g of Black SFP, and 100g with Hyacinth Paste Food Colour. Seal each one in a plastic food bag as soon as it is coloured to keep it from drying out.

2 Using the pastes you have just coloured, cover the cake drum in various wavy sections of colour to give the appearance of the ocean. Use a veining tool to add a wavy texture to the paste whilst it is still soft.

3 Trim and level the cake. You would normally fill the cake before shaping but as this cake is essentially flat, you can fill it once the cake has been carved into the '6' shape. Turn the cake upside down and place centrally on the spare cake drum (dust with icing sugar first to ensure that the cake will not stick).

4 Prepare the template on paper, enlarging it to fit your cake if necessary. Place it on the cake and trim away the cake around the template using the small, sharp knife, making sure you cut straight down. Finish by rounding off the top and base edges of the fish also to give it a curved finish.

5 Cut out and trim the fish tail, making sure it is the same height as the fish body. Stick onto the cake with buttercream.

6 Fill the cake with buttercream and jam, sandwich the cake back together and cover the whole cake with a thin layer of buttercream.

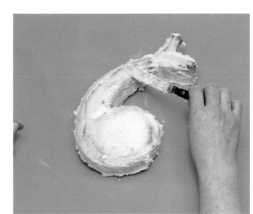

7 Colour 2kg of white sugarpaste with Hydrangea Paste Food Colour then use this to cover the cake. Smooth it around the shape of the '6' with your fingers, gently easing it around the curve of the cake. Around the inside curve (on the '0' part of the figure), gently smooth and stretch the paste. Trim and smooth the paste around the base then polish the top edge of the cake to create a neat finish.

8 When dry, place the cake carefully onto the prepared cake drum, supporting the tail fin as you move it.

top tip

If you are worried about moving the cake with the tail fin attached, place the cake on the drum before you cover it but take care not to cut through the paste on the board when you trim the cake.

9 Colour 300g of MMP for the tail and fins with paste colours in the following proportions: 50g a dark shade of Hydrangea, 100g Hyacinth, 50g Desert Storm, 50g Yucca, and 50g Sunny Lime.

Rub a small amount of white vegetable fat into each colour to soften it then store each colour in a plastic bag to keep it from drying out.

10 Fit the sugar shaper with the large circular hole disc. Push 40g of each of the coloured pastes through the sugar shaper one-by-one to create long strings of each paste. Cut these lengths into shorter sections of 2 x 7cm, 2 x 6cm, and 1 x 5cm in each colour. These will be used to make the fins.

11 Take one set of 'strings', curve the first one into position then attach them side-by-side, one at a time using a fine paintbrush and edible glue. Squeeze the colours slightly then cut off any excess paste with a sharp knife so the shape of the fin is smooth and curved. Trim the base of the fins straight if needed. Repeat this with all the other fins then leave to dry.

12 Once the fins are dry, mark their positions on the cake lightly with the veining tool. When you are happy with the position, make a deeper groove so the fin can sit in the sugarpaste covering, giving it more support. Place some royal icing in a piping bag with a no. 2 nozzle, squeeze a small amount into the groove and

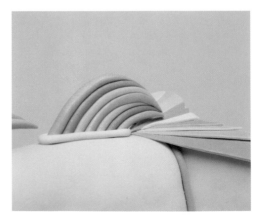

replace the fin. Hold in place until it sets. Repeat with all 5 fins.

13 To neaten the base of each fin, push the remains of the Hydrangea MMP through the sugar shaper and secure these 'strings' to the cake using edible glue.

top tip

If you have any paste left you can use this to neaten the join between the tail fin and the body.

14 To make the tail fin, draw lines from a central point on the template to make various triangular shapes.

15 Roll out some MMP fairly thinly in the first colour of your choice, then cut off the first triangle from the tail fin template and cut this out of the rolled paste. Continue doing this until you have cut out all the triangles. Leave them to dry flat.

16 Once the triangles are dry, assemble them on top of the cake fin with all the points coming together under the final body fin. Secure with dots of royal icing.

17 To make the face, push the remaining Hyacinth MMP through the sugar shaper to form a long string of paste. Cut this in half and lay both lengths together. Cutting through both strings, cut three lengths measuring 12cm, 10cm and 8cm. Coil one end of each one to make the hair and secure in place with edible glue.

18 Cut out the eyes from MMP or SFP in 3 sections – white, blue and black – and secure in place with dots of royal icing. Make a nose and mouth from Hyacinth MMP and secure to the cake with dots of royal icing.

number 4 frog pond

edibles

28cm x 15cm (11" x 6") rectangular sponge cake

Sugarpaste: 2kg (4lb 6½oz) white

1.2kg (2lb 11oz) buttercream

SK Mexican Modelling Paste (MMP): 600g (1lb 5¼oz) White

SK Double Strength Professional Paste Food Colours: Berberis, Holly/Ivy, Hyacinth, Jet Black

SK Professional Designer Paste Food Colour: Sunny Lime

Small amount royal icing

equipment

25.5cm (10") square cake drum

Blossom plunger cutter (PME)

Stylised Flower Cutters: set of 4 (Lindy's Cakes)

In addition to the edibles and equipment listed here, you will also need some basics before starting the project:

Edibles, see pages 10 to 11.

Equipment for Baking and Carving, see pages 6 to 7.

Equipment for Cake Decorating, see pages 8 to 9.

1 Make a rectangular template measuring 5cm x 25.5cm. Cut 2 lengths of cake using the template. Trim off the crusts at the ends using the small knife. Cut 1 of the 2 lengths in half, and 1 of the 2 halves in half again.

2 Round off the edges of the cakes at the top and base. Cut the each of the prepared pieces of cake in half widthways with the large knife and fill with buttercream.

3 Colour 400g of white sugarpaste with Hyacinth Paste Food Colour. Knead in the colour but leave some streaks of blue to represent the water. Cover the cake drum using this paste then leave to dry.

4 Once the drum is dry, position the pieces of cake on it to create the '4' shape. When you are happy with the position, secure them to each other and to the cake drum with a small amount of

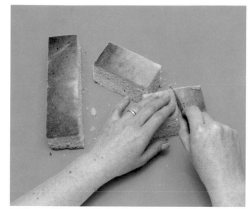

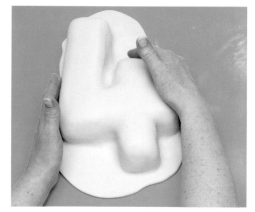

buttercream, taking care not to damage the drum covering.

5 Carefully cover the cake with buttercream. Colour the remaining paste with Hyacinth Paste Food Colour and blend completely so that there are no streaks. Roll out the sugarpaste and place carefully over the cake. Work with the flat of your hand to smooth the paste onto the cake, taking care not to poke it with your fingers. Use a smooth pad of paste to smooth the cake covering and accentuate the shape.

top tip

Take care around the 2 shortest pieces of cake: don't pull the paste to try and get into all the corners, use the pad of paste to define the shape.

6 Cut off the excess sugarpaste and use a cake smoother to neaten around the base of the cake. Be careful not to mark the covering on the cake drum. Finish off the base of the cake using the pad of paste. Finally, polish the whole cake with the pad of paste to remove any blemishes.

7 Colour 200g of White MMP with Holly/Ivy Paste Food Colour, pinch off a small amount and add a little White MMP to this to give 2 shades of green. Colour 200g with Sunny Lime Paste Food Colour, and 50g with Berberis Paste Food Colour but pinch off 2 small amounts so you end up with 3 different shades for the flowers. Finally, colour a small amount of MMP with Jet Black Paste Food Colour.

8 Make 4 frogs from either shade of the green paste, getting progressively smaller each time. For each one roll a large ball for the body, 2 arms, 2 legs, a small ball for the head, 2 very small green balls for the eye sockets and 2 tiny black eyes.

9 Use a craft knife to imprint a mouth and then indent either side of the mouth with the small end of a ball tool. Use the same end of the tool to indent the eye sockets into the two small, green balls.

10 Assemble the frogs, using edible glue to stick the pieces together. Stick the black

eyes into the sockets. Secure the frogs to the cake using edible glue, starting with the largest at the back.

11 Using the remaining green paste and the largest flower cutter, cut out plants to decorate the cake. Place the shapes on a foam pad and draw the veining tool along the length of each one to bend the sides and give them more shape. Attach the plants to the side of the cake in a random pattern, interspersing them with small balls of green paste.

12 Roll out the different shades of Berberis coloured paste and cut out the flowers using the plunger cutter. Transfer the flowers to a foam pad and press into each one with the ball tool to cup the flowers.

13 Colour a little royal icing pale yellow by adding a tiny amount of Berberis Paste Food Colour. Place a no. 2 piping nozzle in a piping bag and fill with the yellow icing. Use this to attach the flowers to the plants, then pipe a centre onto each of the flowers. The same royal icing can be used to pipe an inscription onto the cake drum to finish the cake.

football

edibles

3 x 15cm (6") round sponge cakes

400g (14oz) buttercream

Sugarpaste: 1.8kg (4lb) white

SK Mexican Modelling Paste (MMP): 400g (14oz) Black, 500g (1lb 1oz) White

SK Sugar Florist Paste (SFP): 100g (3oz) White

SK Double Strength Professional Paste Food Colour: Marigold

equipment

23cm (9") square cake drum

Football cutters (Kit Box)

15cm (6") dowelling rod

Textured rolling pin (horizontal lines)

In addition to the edibles and equipment listed here, you will also need some basics before starting the project:

Edibles, see pages 10 to 11.

Equipment for Baking and Carving, see pages 6 to 7.

Equipment for Cake Decorating, see pages 8 to 9.

1 Colour 1kg of white sugarpaste with Marigold Paste Food Colour to make a pale golden yellow. Cover the cake drum and seal the trimmings in a plastic food bag to use later.

2 Level and fill the cakes then stick them together in one large block. Push a 15cm dowelling rod through the cakes from the top: this gives you a height guide when trimming the cake. Start trimming them into a ball shape: cut the corner sections off first with a large knife to get the general shape, then use a small knife to gradually create the ball shape. When you have finished, take the dowelling rod out of the cake.

3 Cover the finished cake with a layer of buttercream then roll out 500g of white sugarpaste and cover the cake, gently moulding the paste around the cake. Cut off the excess from the bottom and then smooth over the cake using a pad of this paste. Make sure there are no bumps or wrinkles that could show through onto the next layer. Leave to dry then place the cake onto the prepared cake drum.

4 Roll out a small amount of the Black MMP between spacers to make sure that each shape is exactly the same thickness. Cut out a pentagon using the football cutter set. Stick this on the top of the cake using edible glue. Cut out white hexagons following the same procedure and stick them in position on the ball: each black pentagon is surrounded by white hexagons and there is one white hexagon between each black shape. Work down as far as you want to go,

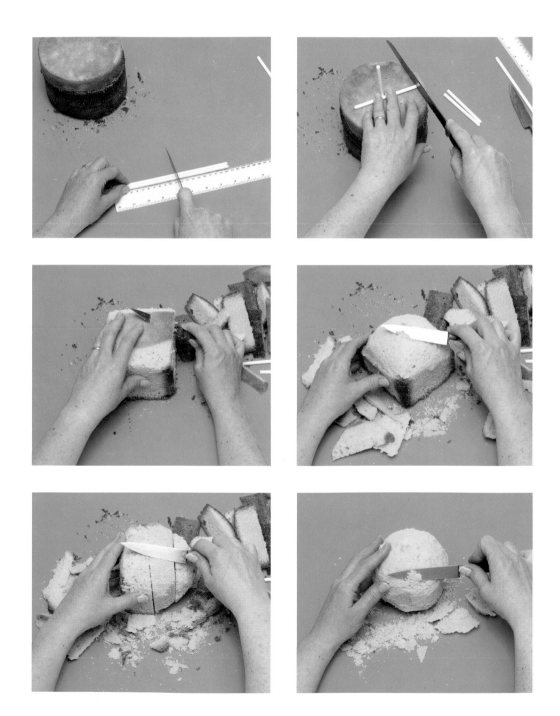

making sure that each shape follows the correct pattern.

5 Colour the remaining white sugarpaste with Marigold Paste Food Colour to make a bright yellow scarf. Roll out the paste into a long sausage between the spacers, then use the textured rolling pin to texture the paste in one direction, turn the paste 90° and texture again. This will give a crisscross effect on the paste to look like knitting.

top tip

The scarf doesn't have to be yellow: you can change the colour to match the recipient's favourite football team.

6 Trim the scarf to measure 5cm in width. Prepare the base of the cake by brushing the area the scarf is to touch with edible glue. Position the scarf in place.

7 Gather the remnants of paste from the scarf and add a little white vegetable fat to soften the paste. Fit a sugar shaper with the multi-hole disc and extrude long lengths of paste. Fold each one in half and pinch the paste together approximately 5mm from the fold. Finish off with a strand or 2 of paste over the pinch. Position the tassels on the edge of the scarf and secure with edible glue.

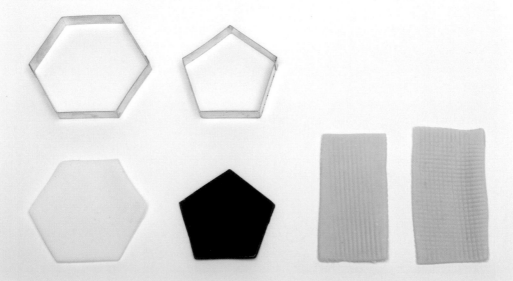

hairy spider

edibles

25.5cm and 15cm (10" and 6") round sponge cakes

2.4kg (5lb 4¾oz) buttercream

Sugarpaste: 1kg (2lb 3¼oz) black, 400g (14¼oz) white

SK Mexican Modelling Paste (MMP): 460g (1lb¼oz) Black, 100g (3½oz) White

SK Double Strength Professional Paste Food Colour: Daffodil

Small amount royal icing

equipment

Cobweb template (see page 88)

25.5cm (10") round cake drum

16 x 22-gauge floral wires

Floral tape: black

4 posy picks: small

Scriber

In addition to the edibles and equipment listed here, you will also need some basics before starting the project:

Edibles, see pages 10 to 11.

Equipment for Baking and Carving, see pages 6 to 7.

Equipment for Cake Decorating, see pages 8 to 9.

1 Cover the cake drum using 400g of white sugarpaste. Leave to dry.

2 Prepare the cobweb template by tracing the pattern onto tracing paper. Once the covered drum is dry, place the template onto the drum and trace over the top of the lines with a scriber to mark the paste, carefully working your way around the web.

3 Add a little white vegetable fat to 100g of Black MMP and work it in well to soften the paste. Fit the sugar shaper with the medium, single-hole disc and fill with the softened paste. Extrude the paste in a long string and cut to the required lengths to cover the straight lines on the cake drum. Secure the lengths in place using edible glue. To neaten the ends of the web that are at the drum edge, roll little balls of black paste and secure them on top with edible glue. Fill in the curved lines on the web: aim to make each one with a long piece of paste and allow the paste to fall over the straight lines. Secure with edible glue and leave to dry.

4 Cut the 25.5cm square cake into 4 x 12.5cm cakes. Cut a 10cm square and 2 x 5cm squares from the 15cm cake.

5 To make the abdomen, level 3 of the 12.5cm cakes and stack them up. The full height should be around 10cm so trim them further if needed then stick them together with buttercream. Shape the cake to make the abdomen: make a basic sphere (see step-by-

step pictures on page 43) but trim one end flatter (this will butt against the body section) and shape the other end to a point. Cover the outside of the finished shape with buttercream. Roll out 500g of black sugarpaste and cover the abdomen. Once covered, use the veining tool to score the surface lengthways. Place on a spare cake drum to dry.

6 Make the body from the 10cm cake and the remaining 12.5cm cake. Trim the larger cake down to 10cm and trim both cakes so they are level. Stack the cakes: the height needs to be 7.5cm so trim if necessary. Stick the cakes together with buttercream and then trim the cake to make an oval shape for the body. Cover with buttercream then cover with 300g of black sugarpaste. Score the surface as before but work downwards from a central point on the top of the body.

7 Level the 5cm cakes, stack and trim to 7.5cm in height if necessary. Stick them together and trim into a ball shape for the head. Cover with 100g of black sugarpaste and score with a scriber from a central point on the top of the head. Leave to dry on a spare cake drum.

8 Make 2 eyes from remnants of the black sugarpaste and secure them in place on the front of the head with edible glue. Fit a piping bag with a no. 1.5 nozzle, fill with royal icing and pipe a white eyeball on each eye. Finish off the eyes with 2 very small pupils made from black sugarpaste.

9 Soften 200g of Black MMP by kneading some white fat into it. Place this into the sugar shaper with the multi-hole disc. Cover the abdomen with the strands of paste, securing them in place with edible glue. Lay the strands along the length of the abdomen, covering it entirely and go as far down the side and under the abdomen as you can. Position the abdomen on the spider web so the flat end is in the centre of the web.

10 Cover the body in the same way but this time arrange the strands following the scored lines, coming from a central point on the top of the body. Again, go down as far as you can. Position this firmly up against the abdomen on the web.

11 Cover the head in the same way, allowing the strands to fall down either side of the eyes, like hair: you can give him a centre parting and a beard if you like! Position this firmly up against the body on the web.

12 Make the 8 legs using 2 of the 20-gauge wires for each one, bound together with black floral tape. Cover each leg in a layer of Black MMP then bend a knee and flatten out one end to create a foot. Pinch 4 sections of each leg from foot to knee to add hair to later on.

13 Insert 2 small posy picks into each side of the body section of the spider, insert 2 legs into each one and position the legs upright on the web. Secure with edible glue or a dot of royal icing.

14 Change the paste in the sugar shaper for 100g of softened Daffodil coloured MMP and extrude short strands of paste to go onto the body of the spider and on each section of leg, like a tassle. Finish off the spider with more very short, black strands on the body and more black strands on the leg sections.

shaggy dog

edibles

20.5cm (8") round sponge cake

400g (14¼oz) buttercream

1kg (2lb 3¼oz) white sugarpaste

SK Mexican Modelling Paste (MMP): 100g (3½oz) Black, 500g (1lb 1½oz) Cream, 500g (1lb 1½oz) Flesh, 500g (1lb 1½oz) Teddy Bear Brown

SK Double Strength Professional Paste Food Colours: Fern, Teddy Bear Brown

equipment

25.5cm (10") round cake drum

Dog template (see page 88)

Flower shaping tool (PME)

In addition to the edibles and equipment listed here, you will also need some basics before starting the project:

Edibles, see pages 10 to 11.

Equipment for Baking and Carving, see pages 6 to 7.

Equipment for Cake Decorating, see pages 8 to 9.

1 Colour 400g of white sugarpaste with Fern Paste Food Colour and cover the cake drum. Cut away a small amount from around the edge of the drum using a small knife to give it a wavy edge. Replace this with a small amount of sugarpaste coloured with Teddy Bear Brown Paste Food Colour and leave to dry.

2 Trim and level the cake and place on a spare cake drum. With the cake sitting on its base, cut a 'v' shaped piece slightly below the central line. Turn the cake over and press down on the cake slightly to flatten the 'v' shape a little more. This makes a concave shape for the bridge of the nose and accentuates the dog's muzzle.

3 Slice the cake in half, fill with buttercream and replace the top half. Start shaping the head by trimming cake away from the cheek areas on both sides of the head, narrowing and accentuating the size of the muzzle. Trim the muzzle so the sharp edges are cut away, softening the whole shape but not reducing the size.

4 Next, trim the eye area by taking off the sharp edges but maintaining the brow. Indent the eyes with your thumb. Trim the nose shape, extending it back towards the corner of the eye. Trim off the edges of the cake around the base.

5 Build up the bridge of the nose a little with remnants of the sugarpaste. Cover the cake with a thin layer of buttercream, roll out the remaining white sugarpaste and cover the whole cake. Smooth the paste with a pad of the same

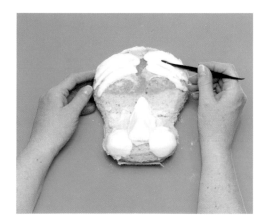

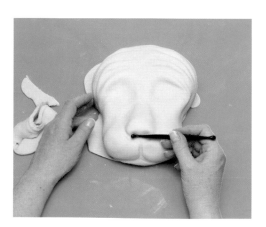

paste, making sure that you keep the shapes you have created.

6 Thickly roll out 40g of Cream MMP into a rectangular shape. Use the pointed end of a flower shaping tool to texture the paste, drawing it over the surface several times to give a rough, furry appearance. Attach this over the nose section using edible glue.

7 Save 50g of the Cream and Flesh MMP. Using the remaining paste, make tufts of fur to cover the cake: pinch off a piece of paste and roll between your fingers and palm to make an elongated teardrop. Press a flower shaping tool down the length of the teardrop, starting at the wide end. Secure the tufts to the cake with edible glue, using Teddy Bear Brown MMP on the muzzle, a band of Flesh MMP on either side, then Cream MMP up to the eyes. On one side the Flesh colour continues up to the brow level whilst on the other side the Teddy Bear Brown starts again.

top tip

Where the colours join, overlap one over the other to make sure that the whole head is covered.

8 Use a little Black MMP to make tiny fur tufts around the nose. Shape the nose from the remaining paste and secure the tufts and nose in position.

9 Shape the ears from the reserved Flesh and Cream MMP, texturing it in the same way as the bridge of the nose. Fold one end over and attach this end to the head using edible glue.

10 Shape the eyes using the remaining white sugarpaste and the Teddy Bear Brown and Black MMP. Stick them together and secure to the head using edible glue.

daisy the cow

edibles

25.5cm x 20.5cm (10" x 8") rectangular sponge cake

Sugarpaste: 2.6kg (5lb 11½oz) white

600g (1lb 5¼oz) buttercream

SK Mexican Modelling Paste (MMP): 150g (5¼oz) Black, 400g (14¼oz) White

SK Sugar Florist Paste (SFP): 100g (3½oz) Marigold

SK Professional Designer Paste Food Colour: Sunny Lime

SK Double Strength Professional Paste Food Colour: Teddy Bear Brown

SK Bridal Satin Lustre Dust Food Colour: Chiffon Pink

SK Professional Metallic Lustre Dust Food Colour: Snowflake

Small amount royal icing

equipment

25.5cm (10") round cake drum

Cow head and eye templates (see page 89)

Flower shaping tool (PME)

Petal cutter: F6 (Orchard Products)

In addition to the edibles and equipment listed here, you will also need some basics before starting the project:

Edibles, see pages 10 to 11.

Equipment for Baking and Carving, see pages 6 to 7.

Equipment for Cake Decorating, see pages 8 to 9.

1 Colour 400g of sugarpaste with Sunny Lime Paste Food Colour and cover the cake drum. Leave to dry.

2 Place the cake on a spare cake drum. Level the top, cut a layer in the cake and fill with buttercream. Make the cow template then place this on the cake and cut out the shape using a small knife. Make sure that you cut straight down. Trim away the edges of the cake, softening the shape and making it more curved.

3 To make the face, cut away a curved section below the eyes in front of the nose. Using a small amount of buttercream, stick a pad of paste in the eyebrow area and nose area to accentuate the shape of the face. Smooth the edges of the pads so they don't show through the final covering of paste. Trim either side of the face to make it narrower then undercut around the base of the cake. Finally, press your fingers into the sponge to indent the eye socket area.

4 Cover the cake with a thin layer of buttercream. Roll out 2kg of white sugarpaste and cover the cake. Use a pad of the sugarpaste to smooth over the cake, indenting and accentuating the carved shape, especially around the eyes. Cut away any excess sugarpaste and continue to smooth around the base of the cake with the pad of paste.

5 Indent the paste to create the mouth using a veining tool. Use the flatter end of a flower shaping tool to indent the paste for the nostrils,

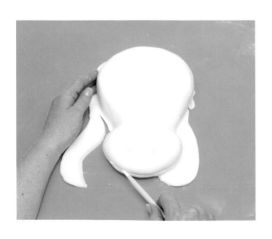

then use your fingers to smooth and shape them. Make the blotches on the cow with Black MMP and secure in place with edible glue.

6 Shape the ears from 100g of sugarpaste. Roll out the paste thickly, cut a rough ear shape using a pizza wheel, then use your fingers to soften the edges of the ear. Cut one end flat to attach to the head, then soften the other end of the ear and make the tip thinner. Repeat to make a second ear than attach to either side of the head using edible glue. Dust the inside of each ear using Chiffon Pink and Snowflake Lustre Dusts: tap a little of the dust out onto kitchen roll and use a dry, flat paintbrush to dust the ears a little at a time.

7 To make the horns, colour 100g of MMP with Teddy Bear Brown Paste Food Colour. Shape into 2 horns and leave to dry until they can hold their shape. Attach to the head above the ears using a small amount of royal icing, then support until dry using a folded piece of kitchen roll.

8 Cut out the eyes using the templates and secure in place using edible glue. Make the eyelashes by rolling very small pieces of Black MMP between your fingers, curl them then attach in place with small dots of edible glue.

9 Roll out the Marigold SFP and cut out a large blossom. Soften and frill the edges of the blossom on a foam pad using a bone tool and leave to dry. Once dry, secure the flower to the mouth of the cow using royal icing.

building blocks

edibles

25.5cm x 30.5cm (10" x 12") rectangular sponge cake (at least 7.5cm (3") deep)

Sugarpaste: 3kg (6lb 9¾oz) white

500g (1lb 1½oz) buttercream

SK Mexican Modelling Paste (MMP): small amount Black, 300g (10½oz) White

SK Sugar Florist Paste (SFP): 100g (3½oz) White

SK Double Strength Professional Paste Food Colours: Daffodil, Hyacinth, Marigold, Peach, Rose, Teddy Bear Brown

SK Designer Professional Paste Food Colours: Desert Storm, Yucca

Small amount royal icing

equipment

Train and teddy templates (see page 89)

25.5cm (10") square cake drum

Mini spacers (Kit Box)

Circle cutters: set of 11

Flower shaping tool (PME)

Number cutter set (Patchwork Cutters)

SK Great Impressions Rattle Mould

Boat embosser (FMM)

Primrose cutter: small (FMM)

In addition to the edibles and equipment listed here, you will also need some basics before starting the project:

Edibles, see pages 10 to 11.

Equipment for Baking and Carving, see pages 6 to 7.

Equipment for Cake Decorating, see pages 8 to 9.

1 Cover the cake drum with 400g of white sugarpaste and leave to one side to dry.

2 Trim the top of the cake flat then use a ruler and a small knife to trim the crust from either side of the cake. Cut the cake into squares as follows: 2 x 12.5cm, 1 x 10cm, 1 x 7.5cm, and 3 x 5cm. Cut smoothly through the cake ensuring that the blade of the knife is cutting straight down and not undercutting the cake.

3 Stack the 2 x 12.5cm cakes on top of each other and use the ruler to measure a depth of 12.5cm. Cut the cake to this height, making a 12.5cm cube. Use the remnants of this cake to increase the height of the 10cm cake, making it into a cube. Trim the other cakes into cubes.

4 Fill the cakes and stick all the layers back together. Place the cakes onto a spare cake drum ready for covering (don't crumb-coat the cakes with buttercream yet). Cover with cling film to stop them drying out.

5 Cover the largest cake first. Colour 600g of white sugarpaste with SK Yucca Paste Food Colour to a soft blue shade. Roll out a quarter of the paste at a time between spacers, keeping the rest sealed in a plastic bag. Use a cutting wheel to trim the bottom of the paste: this will be the bottom of the block.

6 Cover the first side of the cake with buttercream and apply the prepared paste to the block with the trimmed side neatly positioned

at the base. Use the cake smoother to press the paste very gently, helping it stick to the cake. Hold the paste in place with the smoother and, using a small knife, cut against the smoother to trim the edges. Work your way around the block to cover each side.

7 Colour the following quantities of white sugarpaste for the remaining blocks: 500g Rose, 200g Daffodil, 550g Hyacinth, and 500g Desert Storm. Keep them all sealed in plastic bags until needed. Cover all the blocks the same way, using spacers to ensure you get the same depth of paste each time. Leave to dry.

8 Colour small amounts of SFP with the same colours as the sugarpaste. Roll out one colour at a time between a pair of mini spacers to give you a depth of approximately 2-3mm, cut a narrow strip using a ribbon cutter and secure to the edges of the blocks to neaten the joins. Start with the top and bottom edges, then choose which will be the front of the block and run a ribbon of paste vertically along each edge. Use edible glue to

secure each strip in place. You should be able to handle the blocks without marking them if the sugarpaste is dry. Choose colours to complement the colours of the bricks, following the photograph as a guide.

9 Decorate each block with your chosen designs using the coloured SFP and various cutters. Place some royal icing into a piping bag with a no. 1 nozzle and secure each design in place using dots of icing. Cut out the numbers and attach them in the same way.

10 Follow the templates and step photographs to cut out the train and the teddy bear. Repeat the pattern on all 4 sides of each block.

11 Stack the blocks on the prepared cake drum. When you are happy with their position, use royal icing to secure them in place. Model a rabbit from White MMP, following the step photograph as a guide. Position the rabbit on one of the blocks and secure him in place with royal icing.

roll the dice

edibles

2 x 18cm (7") square sponge cakes (sufficient depth to give a trimmed height of 15cm (6") when stacked)

Sugarpaste: 400g (14¼oz) black, 1kg (2lb 3¼oz) white

450g (1lb) buttercream

SK Mexican Modelling Paste (MMP): 200g (7¼oz) Black, 100g (3½oz) White

SK Double Strength Professional Paste Food Colour: Poinsettia

SK Professional Metallic Lustre Dust Food Colour: Light Gold

Small amount royal icing

equipment

20.5cm (8") square cake drum

Heart plunger cutter: small

Circle cutter: no. 5 (FMM)

In addition to the edibles and equipment listed here, you will also need some basics before starting the project:

Edibles, see pages 10 to 11.

Equipment for Baking and Carving, see pages 6 to 7.

Equipment for Cake Decorating, see pages 8 to 9.

top tip

If you are making more than one dice, it is more economical to make the cake as a 35.5cm (14") square and cut from there. If you don't have 2 18cm (7") cake tins, a larger tin can be used – I cut 2 cakes from a 35.5cm (14") tin. Remember to adjust the amount of cake mixture and covering to suit the cake size (see pages 15 and 30).

1 Cover the cake drum with the black sugarpaste and leave to one side to dry.

2 Trim the top of the cake flat. Using a ruler and small knife, measure the cake to 15cm (this is best done by trimming off the crusty edges from either side of the cake). Mark the cake on both sides then use a long, serrated knife to cut smoothly through the cake, ensuring that the blade of the knife is cutting straight down and not undercutting the cake. Continue trimming away until you have a neat 15cm square.

3 Cut a layer in each cake then fill the cakes and stack the layers together to make a cube. Place the cake onto a spare cake drum and cover with buttercream.

4 Colour 1kg of white sugarpaste with Poinsettia Paste Food Colour and cover the cake. As this cake is tall you will need to take extra care when covering the sides: allow the paste to flop down the sides and very carefully ease the paste onto the cake, making sure that there are

no creases. Trim and smooth the sugarpaste to make a neat finish.

5 Whilst the paste is still soft, use the larger end of the ball tool to indent the paste ready for inserting the dots on the dice. The 2 opposite sides of a dice add up to 7. Roll large balls of Black MMP and glue into the indentations on the dice using edible glue. Allow to dry.

6 Prepare a rectangular template for the playing card measuring 12cm x 7cm. Trim off the corners. Roll out 100g of White SFP quite thinly and cut out 2 cards: use the pizza wheel to cut straight sides, then use a craft knife to cut the curved corners. Leave to dry on a flat surface.

7 Colour 10g of the white trimmings from the cards with Poinsettia Paste Food Colour. Roll out the red paste and cut out 4 capital letter 'A's using the craft knife and 2 hearts using the plunger cutter. Stick an 'A' and a heart to the top-left corner of each card. Use Black MMP and the craft knife to make two more 'A's and 2 club or spade shapes and glue in place. Leave to dry.

8 Place a small amount of royal icing into a piping bag with a no. 2 nozzle. Offset the cards one on top of the other so you can see the letters and secure in place with dots of royal icing. Place the cake on top of the cards, leaving the lettered corners showing, and secure in place with dots of royal icing.

9 Thickly roll out the remnants of the White SFP and cut out several poker chips using the circle cutter. Leave to dry then paint with Light Gold Metallic Lustre Dust Food Colour mixed with clear alcohol. Leave to dry, then attach them to the corner of the cake drum using dots of royal icing.

top tip

If you would like to add an inscription, use a slightly larger cake drum, either round or rectangular, and pipe your message in front of the cake.

christmas figurines

edibles

25.5cm (10") square sponge cake

Sugarpaste: 750g (1lb 10½oz) white

400g (14¼oz) buttercream

SK Mexican Modelling Paste (MMP): 500g (1lb 1½oz) White

SK Sugar Florist Paste (SFP): 150g (5¼oz) White

SK Double Strength Professional Paste Food Colours: Chestnut, Cyclamen, Fern, Holly/Ivy, Hyacinth, Hydrangea, Marigold, Poinsettia

SK Professional Designer Paste Food Colour: Jet Black

SK Professional Metallic Lustre Dust Food Colours: Classic Gold, Snowflake

Sugar sticks (see page 9) or dried spaghetti

Small amount royal icing

equipment

Father Christmas' coat, cape and angel wing templates (see page 90)

3 x 7.5cm (3") round cake cards

7.5cm (3") round cutter

3 x 5cm (2") dowelling rods

Texture mat (or new, clean pan scourer)

In addition to the edibles and equipment listed here, you will also need some basics before starting the project:

Edibles, see pages 10 to 11.

Equipment for Baking and Carving, see pages 6 to 7.

Equipment for Cake Decorating, see pages 8 to 9.

1 Level the top of the cake using a large knife, then cut out 9 x 7.5cm circles (3 for each cone). Cut each mini cake in half and fill with buttercream.

2 Stack three cakes on top of each other and push a dowelling rod down the centre of each stack: this supports the top and makes it easier to cut to shape. Use a small knife to shape the cakes into cones, trimming away just a little at a time to make sure you don't spoil the shape.

3 Once you are happy with the shape, sandwich the cake layers together with buttercream then use a little more buttercream to stick each cake onto a cake card. Cover the cakes with buttercream.

4 Roll out 250g of white sugarpaste and cover each cone. Follow the individual instructions below to decorate the Christmas tree, angel and Father Christmas.

father christmas

1 Mix together 150g of white sugarpaste and 100g of White MMP, then colour the paste with Poinsettia Paste Food Colour.

2 Roll out 50g of the red paste into a rectangle and stick this to the front of the cone at the base using edible glue. This is the only area that will show from this layer. Make sure the edges are rolled thinly so they don't show through the next layer.

3 Roll out 100g of the red paste and cut out the coat using the template. Secure this to the cone with edible glue.

4 Roll 20g of White MMP into a small sausage shape for the fur trim on the coat. Roll it over the texture mat (or pan scourer) to roughen the surface then attach it to the coat with edible glue, from waist level downwards, all the way round the back of the figure and up to the waist level again. Press the flat end of the veining tool into the paste to help it stick and to add texture.

5 Make 2 arms from 50g of the red paste, bend slightly at the elbows and flatten the hand end of the arm to represent the long cuffs on Father Christmas' coat. Secure the arms at the shoulders to the cone shape (don't flatten the arms at the shoulders).

6 Roll 2 cuffs from White MMP, texture as before and attach with edible glue using the flat end of the veining tool again.

7 Colour 60g of White MMP with Chestnut Paste Food Colour to a light flesh tone. Make 2 hands from 10g of this paste, push a sugar stick or dried spaghetti into the wrist of each hand and attach to the arms with edible glue.

8 Roll out 50g of red paste and use the template to cut out the cape. Secure this to the neck area of the cone, allowing it to drape over the shoulders. Trim the cape with fur as before.

9 Using the remaining flesh coloured MMP (except for a small pinch for the nose) model a head and gently push this over the dowelling rod. Secure with a little edible glue if necessary. Indent the eyes with the end of a piping nozzle. Attach the nose with edible glue. Colour a small amount of paste black, roll 2 eyes and stick them to the face with edible glue.

10 Roll a hat from the remaining red paste and attach to the head with edible glue. Push a small sugar stick into the end of the hat and attach a white ball of sugarpaste for the pompom. Make a length of fur trim to go around the base of the hat.

11 Make a moustache and beard from White MMP and attach in place with edible glue.

angel

top tip

Make sure you start working on this figure with the paste join at the back.

1 Make a paste by mixing Snowflake Metallic Lustre Dust with clear alcohol and paint this all over the cone. Leave to dry.

2 Colour 150g of White MMP with Hydrangea Paste Food Colour to make a pale blue. Roll out and cut out a rough triangular shape for the angel gown. Attach to the front and sides of the cone using edible glue, smoothing the edges flat against the shape.

3 Colour 120g of White SFP with Marigold Paste Food Colour. Take off 20g and roll out thinly. Cut a strip of paste using the ribbon cutter with the small wheel and attach along the edges of the gown with edible glue. If there are any joins in the paste, position them where they can't be seen, such as where the hands will be.

4 Use the remaining pale blue paste to make 2 sleeves. Make the hand end flatter and secure to the shoulders with edible glue, making sure the shoulders don't bulge out.

5 Colour 60g of White MMP with Chestnut Paste Food Colour to a light flesh tone. Make 2 hands from 10g of this paste and attach to the sleeves with a short sugar stick and a little edible glue.

6 Roll out the remaining 100g of Marigold coloured SFP and cut out 2 wings from the template. Leave on a flat surface to dry. Paint with a colour wash made from clear alcohol and Classic Gold Metallic Lustre Dust. Once dry, position them so they stand out on either side of the angel and secure with a few dots of royal icing.

7 Pinch off enough flesh coloured paste for a nose and 2 ears then roll the remaining paste into a head shape and attach onto the top of the cone with a little edible glue or royal icing. Use the narrow end of a no. 1.5 piping nozzle to indent the eyes, then use the wide end to indent the smiling mouth. Attach the nose and ears using a tiny dot of edible glue. Make and attach the eyes in the same way as for Father Christmas.

8 Colour 50g of MMP with Marigold Paste Food Colour. Add a small amount of white fat to soften the paste and extrude through the sugar shaper to create strands of hair. Attach them neatly with edible glue, draping the hair around the side of the head and creating a bun at the back.

9 Make the halo for the head in the same way as the strips around the gown and secure in place with edible glue. Paint this and the strips on the gown with a mixture of clear alcohol and Classic Gold Metallic Lustre Dust.

christmas tree

1 Colour 50g of White SFP with Jet Black Paste Food Colour. Model into a bucket shape around 5cm tall for the base of the Christmas tree and leave to dry. Once dry, attach to the base of the final cone with royal icing.

2 Colour 100g of White MMP with Holly/Ivy Paste Food Colour and 100g with Fern. Take half of the Holly/Ivy paste and model a rough sausage that will cover the width of the cone base. Roll over it with the rolling pin to broaden it slightly. Use the flat end of the veining tool to create branches from one long side of the sausage. Flatten the other long side much more so it will sit flush with the side of the cone. Secure it to the tree with royal icing, allowing it to hang down from the bottom of the cone.

3 Use the fern coloured paste next to make more branches in the same way. Attach to the cone so that the branches overlap the previous colour. Continue this all the way up the tree, alternating the colours. On finishing the final section, wrap it round the cone and pinch it to a point at the top.

4 Colour small amounts of MMP with Hyacinth, Cyclamen and Marigold Paste Food Colours to make the baubles and the star and attach them to the tree with dots of royal icing. If extra support is needed, use small sugar sticks.

5 To finish the tree, make a very thin sausage of White MMP, texture it using the texture mat and then drape it over the tree like tinsel, using dots of royal icing to secure it in place.

6 Paint the orange baubles and the star with clear alcohol mixed with Classic Gold Metallic Lustre Dust. Dust the other baubles and the tinsel with Snowflake Metallic Lustre Dust.

magician's hat

edibles

25.5cm x 30.5cm (10" x 12") rectangular
sponge cake

340g (12oz) buttercream

Sugarpaste: 400g (14¼oz) black, 2kg (4lb
6½oz) white

SK Sugar Florist Paste (SFP): 300g
(10½oz) White

SK Double Strength Professional Paste
Food Colours: Chestnut, Wisteria

SK Professional Designer Paste Food
Colour: Jet Black

SK Professional Metallic Lustre Dust Food
Colours: Classic Gold, Snowflake

SK Edible Paint: Gold

equipment

25.5cm (10") round cake drum

2 dowelling rods

Square, circle and star cutters, various
sizes (Kit Box)

In addition to the edibles and equipment listed here, you
will also need some basics before starting the project:

Edibles, see pages 10 to 11.

Equipment for Baking and Carving, see pages 6 to 7.

Equipment for Cake Decorating, see pages 8 to 9.

1 Cover the cake drum with 400g of black
sugarpaste.

2 Cut the sponge cake into squares measuring
15cm, 12.5cm, 10cm, 7.5cm, 5cm and
2.5cm. Level each square using a long, serrated
knife and a spirit level; the cakes don't need to be
the same depth as each other but must be flat.

3 Shape the squares into circles: you could use
round cutters (if you have any large enough),
plates, or make templates from greaseproof
paper. Once you have carved all 6 circles, stick
the cakes together with buttercream, starting at
the bottom. If you are worried that the stack of
cakes will fall out of shape, push 1 or 2 dowelling
rods down through the centre of the cakes, 1
after the third layer and another when the stack
is complete. Carve down the sides to make a
smooth cone shape. Make a small cone with
sugarpaste to finish off the very top of the hat and

secure in place with edible glue. Cover the cone with buttercream.

4 Colour 2kg of sugarpaste a rich, deep purple using Wisteria Paste Food Colour. Measure the circumference of the base cake using a tape measure (or string and a ruler): this is the width of paste you will need. Roll out the paste into a rough triangular shape. Measure the paste to make sure it is wide enough to go all the way around the base of the cake.

5 Carefully trim the lower edge of the paste straight with the pizza wheel and then apply the paste to the cake with the lower edge lined up around the base of the cake. Press gently to encourage the paste to stick as you work around the cake.

6 Once you have the paste on the cake, use a small, sharp knife to score down the paste where it overlaps. Pull it back slightly, slip one of the smoothers underneath and cut against this down the scored line to remove the excess paste. Gently position the paste back onto the cake and smooth the join closed.

7 Flatten the top of the paste at the point and gently ease it to one side so it bends over. Use a veining tool to add creases. Use cake smoothers to give the paste a smooth finish, then polish with a pad of paste to make it even and silky in appearance. Place the cake onto the prepared cake drum.

8 Roll out the remaining purple paste into a long strip for the brim of the hat, 5cm-7.5cm in width. Trim both long sides straight, then place around the base of the hat, positioning the join at the same place as the join on the hat. Smooth with a pad of paste, then lift up the paste at 2 or 3 points around the brim and push a small pad of kitchen roll underneath to lift the edge slightly. Roll

the trimmings of black sugarpaste into a very long sausage shape, using cake smoothers to create an even width. Attach this to the edge of the brim using edible glue. Allow to dry, then remove the pads of kitchen roll.

9 Colour 200g of SFP with Jet Black Paste Food Colour. Roll out the paste to make a band 4cm wide and as long as required to go around the base of the cake. Trim and attach to the base of the cake using a little edible glue. Smooth it into place using the smoother, but be careful not to damage the brim of the hat at the base of the smoother.

10 Release the band a little from the cake to the front left of the hat so that it bulges out slightly (this will be in the centre of the buckle). Make 4 holes in the hatband from the position of the buckle to represent the buckle holes.

11 Cut a square from the remnants of Jet Black SFP using a large square cutter. Using a smaller square cutter, cut out the centre to create a buckle shape. Paint with Edible Gold Paint and leave to dry. Once dry, position over the bulge in the band and secure with edible glue.

12 Colour 100g of White SFP with Chestnut Paste Food Colour. Using star and circle cutters, cut out several shapes. Turn the circles into moons by using the same circle cutter again and cutting out part of the shape. Paint the stars and moons in the same way as the buckle. Allow to dry then attach to the cake using edible glue.

13 Use a dry, flat brush to dust the surface with Snowflake Dust Food Colour, giving the cake a magical sparkle.

noah's ark

edibles

30.5cm x 25.5cm (12" x 10") rectangular sponge cake

Sugarpaste: 400g (14¼oz) chocolate, 1.6kg (3lb 8½oz) white

500g (1lb 1½oz) buttercream

SK Mexican Modelling Paste (MMP): 100g (3½oz) Black, 500g (1lb 1½oz) White

SK Double Strength Professional Paste Food Colours: Hyacinth, Marigold, Rose, Teddy Bear Brown

Small amount royal icing

SK Piping Gel

equipment

Ark template (see page 90)

25.5cm (10") square cake drum

Circle cutters: 1cm and 2cm (³/₈" and ¾")

Flower shaping tool (PME)

Textured rolling pin

In addition to the edibles and equipment listed here, you will also need some basics before starting the project:

Edibles, see pages 10 to 11.

Equipment for Baking and Carving, see pages 6 to 7.

Equipment for Cake Decorating, see pages 8 to 9.

1 Colour 500g of white sugarpaste with Hyacinth Paste Food Colour but don't blend the colour completely, leave streaks of white paste. Roll this out and cover the cake drum. Leave the drum to dry and place the trimmings in a plastic food bag to use for the waves later.

2 Trace and cut out the ark template. Level the cake top then turn it over and place the template widthways across the cake. Cut the cake in half using the template as a guide: the template will easily fit twice across the cake width leaving a small amount remaining for the cabin.

3 Stack the 2 rectangles on top of each other and secure them together with buttercream. Place the template on top of the stack of cakes and cut out the shape using a large knife. Place the cake on a spare cake drum and keep the template as you will need it later on.

4 Start trimming the side of the cake using a small knife. Trim down the front of the cake, undercutting as you go down to the board to shape the hull of the boat. Do the same down the back of the boat, then shape the side of the boat, again undercutting towards the base of the hull.

5 Cut the top cake in half widthways ready to fill with buttercream. Remove this piece from the cake and spread the top of the cake with buttercream. Trim 1cm off the template (this is the deck size) then place on top of the slice of cake. Cut the template out around the outer oval shape to make the rail around the deck. Place the rail

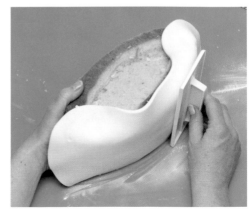

back onto the cake. Cut the lower cake in half widthways and fill with buttercream. Replace it then trim around the edge of the rail using the small knife.

6 Colour 1kg of white sugarpaste with Teddy Bear Brown Paste Food Colour to make a beige colour. Cover 1 side of the cake with buttercream. Roll out the paste between the spacers and trim the bottom edge of the paste straight using the pizza wheel. Position the cut edge on the cake board and press the paste onto the cake using a smoother. Trim the excess from the top and sides and smooth the paste back into place.

7 Measure up the hull and mark at 1cm intervals for the width of the planks. Use the pointed end of the flower shaping tool to mark the planks following the lines. Mark lines horizontally in the same way to show the individual planks.

8 Roll out 200g of chocolate sugarpaste between spacers and cut out the deck template. Insert this inside the rails of the cake. Measure the cake on the inside of the deck rail from the deck to the top of the rail and set a ribbon

cutter to this measurement. Roll out a further 100g of chocolate sugarpaste between spacers, cut out the ribbon and cut to the length required.

9 Cover the cake with a thin layer of buttercream and apply the paste ribbon, allowing the excess width to butt over the outside of the boat. Trim the ends to fit. Repeat on the other side. Measure the top of the rail, add 3mm and cut a paste ribbon in the same way as before.

10 To finish off the hull, cut 2 further strips of ribbon paste the same width as the rail. Apply these to either end of the hull, covering the join in the paste. Allow the excess length to curl over at the top.

11 Using the remnants of cake, cut a rectangular shape measuring 7cm x 5cm x 3cm. Sandwich the pieces together with buttercream if necessary.

12 Cut a prism shaped piece measuring 7cm x 5cm x 2.5cm for the roof. Place this on top of the rectangle to make the cabin, using buttercream to hold it in place.

13 Cover the cabin with buttercream and cover the sides using the remnants of Teddy Bear Brown coloured sugarpaste. Position the cabin onto the deck of the boat and secure with buttercream.

14 Colour the remaining 100g of white sugarpaste with Rose Paste Food Colour, roll out then texture with the ribbed rolling pin. Cut out a 10cm square for the roof, gently fold in half and place on top of the cabin. It should overhang slightly around the edges.

15 Position the ark on the prepared cake drum. Make the waves from the remnants of blue sugarpaste and position them around the ends of the boat, covering up any marks there may be around the cake. Use royal icing to secure the cake in place and to paint over the waves. To add a more watery effect, paint with clear piping gel.

16 Colour a small amount of MMP with Marigold Paste Food Colour. Cut out a circle using the larger of the 2 cutters, then cut out the centre with the smaller cutter to make the porthole frames. Make 6 altogether. Cut 6 smaller circles from Black MMP, attach them to the frames and glue these to the cake and cabin with edible glue.

17 Make the 2 birds from 40g of White MMP. Model a 'comma' shape for the body, flatten the fatter end to make the tail and use the flower shaping tool to mark feathers on the tail. Pinch the opposite end to make a beak. Make 2 teardrop shapes for the wings, texture in the same way as for the tail and attach in place. Paint on the eyes and beak using a fine paintbrush and a touch of Marigold and Teddy Bear Brown Paste Food Colours. Secure the birds to the roof with a dot of royal icing.

18 Colour 20g of White MMP with Teddy Bear Brown Paste Food Colour for the snails. Shape 2 snail bodies from the paste with antennae on the heads. Add a small amount of white to the remnants and roll up the shells. Secure to the bodies using a dot of royal icing and then secure the snails to the rail of the ark.

19 For the elephants, add a little Black MMP to 100g of White MMP to make a pale grey. Shape each head and trunk from 25g of paste.

Use a craft knife to give the trunk wrinkles and shape the tip of the trunk using the craft knife and flower shaping tool. Indent the eye sockets using a ball tool then insert small balls of Black MMP and secure with a dot of royal icing. If you want your elephant to have tusks, shape them from any remnants of white paste and attach with a dot of royal icing. Roll 2 balls of grey paste for the bodies, push these onto the front part of the deck and attach the elephant heads to them using royal icing.

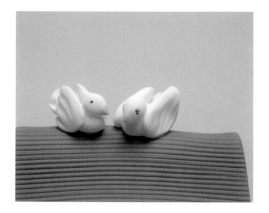

20 To make the hippos, colour 140g of White MMP with a hint of Rose Paste Food Colour. Shape each head from 40g of paste, making the mouth end much larger. Use the craft knife to cut the mouth and the flower shaping tool to open it up a little. Mark the nostrils and eye sockets with the small end of a ball tool. Make 2 larger balls of pink paste for each hippo and indent these for the ears. Roll 2 large balls from the remaining pink paste and position these on the remaining deck space. Attach the heads using royal icing. Attach the ears with a dot of royal icing then fill the eye sockets with Black MMP. Make 8 little teeth and attach them to the mouth using royal icing.

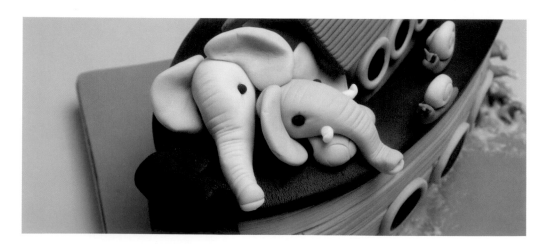

pretty petals

edibles

25.5cm (10") round cake, levelled and trimmed

Sugarpaste: 2.7kg (6lb) white

SK Sugar Florist Paste (SFP): 300g (10½oz) White

100g (3½oz) royal icing

SK Double Strength Professional Paste Food Colours: Daffodil, Fuchsia, Hydrangea, Wisteria

SK Professional Designer Paste Food Colours: Desert Storm, Jet Black

equipment

Flower template (see page 91)

30.5cm (12") round cake drum

Blossom plunger cutters: small, medium and large (PME)

In addition to the edibles and equipment listed here, you will also need some basics before starting the project:

Edibles, see pages 10 to 11.

Equipment for Baking and Carving, see pages 6 to 7.

Equipment for Cake Decorating, see pages 8 to 9.

1 Draw and cut a 23cm circle from tracing/greaseproof paper. Fold in half twice to mark the centre.

2 Colour 400g of white sugarpaste with Desert Storm Paste Food Colour and cover the cake drum.

3 Measure and mark the centre point of the covered cake drum. Place the centre point of the traced circle onto the centre of the cake drum and secure with a sterilized, glass-headed pin.

4 Cut the paste around the edge of the circle using a pizza wheel. Remove the pin and paper, then remove the paste you have just cut off (you may need to use a knife to remove it carefully as it will be stuck to the cake drum).

important note

Put the pin away safely to avoid the risk of it getting into the cake or sugarpaste.

5 Colour 100g of white sugarpaste with Fuchsia Paste Food Colour. Roll out the paste into a long strip to the same thickness as before. Trim one long edge straight with the pizza wheel, then position it over the exposed cake drum. Smooth over the paste carefully to secure it in place, then trim away the excess paste at the join and around the edge with a sharp knife.

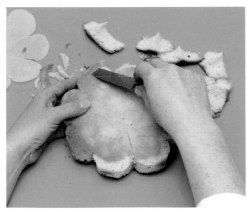
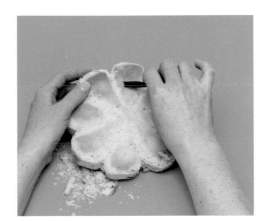
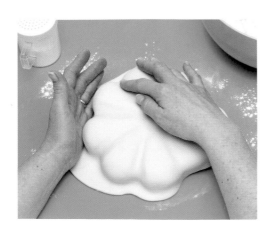

6 Trace the blossom template onto greaseproof paper. You may need to enlarge the shape using a photocopier to suit the size of your cake.

7 Place the template on the cake and cut out the flower shape using a small, sharp knife. Work all the way around until you have cut every petal. Define each petal by indenting the shape right up to the centre of the flower but don't cut too deep otherwise the cake may break apart. Trim off all the edges, including at the base, and define each petal by creating a curved shape.

8 Cut and fill the cake, lining up the petals carefully when you put the top back on. Cover the surface of the cake with a thin layer of buttercream.

9 Colour the remaining white sugarpaste with Wisteria Paste Food Colour, roll out between spacers if you have them and cover the cake. Work around the shape to smooth the paste, defining the petals first with your fingers, then smooth out any lumps or finger marks with a pad of the paste. Work quickly but carefully.

10 Using a quilting tool, make stitch marks along the sides of the petals. Leave the paste covering to dry then position the cake on the finished cake drum.

11 Colour 100g of SFP pale blue using Hydrangea Paste Food Colour. Cut out 3 sizes of blossom using plunger cutters. Press into each blossom on a foam pad using a ball tool: this will lift the edges a little. Leave to dry.

12 Colour half the royal icing with Daffodil Paste Food Colour and the other half with Jet Black Designer Paste Food Colour. Fit 2 piping bags with no. 1.5 nozzles and fill one with each colour of icing. Pipe a snail's trail over the join around the edge of the cake drum.

13 Secure the blossoms to the cake in a scattered pattern with a dot of the yellow royal icing, then pipe a dot of yellow icing into the centre of each flower. Using the other piping bag, pipe a tiny black dot on the yellow centre of each flower and delicate black dots in and around the flowers to accentuate the scattered effect.

charming cat

edibles

25.5cm x 20.5cm (10" x 8") rectangular sponge cake, levelled and trimmed

Sugarpaste: 2.5kg (5lb 8¼oz) white

300g (10½oz) buttercream

SK Mexican Modelling Paste (MMP): small amount Black, 200g (7¼oz) White

SK Double Strength Professional Food Paste Colours: Vine, Violet

equipment

25.5cm (10") square cake drum

Cat template (see page 91)

Fine silver floral wire

In addition to the edibles and equipment listed here, you will also need some basics before starting the project:

Edibles, see pages 10 to 11.

Equipment for Baking and Carving, see pages 6 to 7.

Equipment for Cake Decorating, see pages 8 to 9.

1 Colour 500g (1lb 1½oz) of white sugarpaste with Violet Paste Food Colour. Roll out and cover the cake drum. Leave to dry.

2 Trace all the details from the template onto tracing/greaseproof paper. Cut out the cat, place it onto the cake and cut the cake into shape. Cut through the template following the outline of the legs and head; this gives you a guideline to follow once the template is removed.

3 Cut and fill the cake and place the top layer back into position. Using the small knife, round off the edges around the cat shape and around the feature outlines you have just cut. Shape the cat's legs, head, chest, ears and face. Don't cut too much off at this stage: rounding off the edges slightly will make the features of the cat easier to define later. Work carefully and trim only a little at a time.

top tip

If you trim off a little too much cake, don't worry as it can be stuck back on with buttercream.

4 Continue trimming small pieces of cake away. Focus on the front legs, making them long and elegant. Trim around the front paws. As you work up the legs, allow them to get wider so they blend in where they join the body. Make sure the front leg that is behind is cut to a shallower depth so that it appears further away. Indent the eyes gently

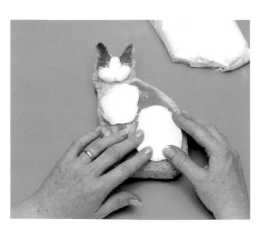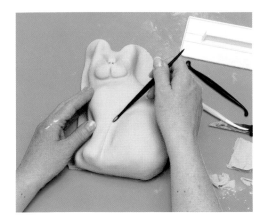

using your fingers and accentuate the shape of the nose. Finally, trim away a small amount of cake around the base of the cat so the sugarpaste can be tucked under.

5 Place the cat onto a spare cake drum. Spread a little buttercream on the cat's face, chest and back leg, then shape small amounts of sugarpaste to go on these areas and pad them out a little. Shape the paste on the face to make the nose and cheeks more rounded. Cover the cake with a thin layer of buttercream.

6 Roll out the remainder of the white sugarpaste between spacers and place over the cat. Working quickly but carefully, smooth the paste over the cat with your fingers, bringing through the features. Trim away the excess paste and tuck the edges under the cat to give it more of a 3D appearance.

7 Use the veining tool and bone tool to accentuate the shapes and to texture the cat. Work smoothly along the legs, define the back legs, then work around the cheeks, chin, eyes and nose. Draw in the mouth with the veining tool. Work on the ears, softening the edges and indenting the inside a little. Texture the paws by drawing 3 delicate lines where the claws would be.

8 Shape a tail from MMP, tapering it at one end. Join the fatter end to the bottom of the cat, tucking it in underneath and securing in place with edible glue. Coil the tapering end around the front and over the back foot, and again secure in place with edible glue.

9 Shape the eyes using trimmings of white sugarpaste coloured green with Vine Paste Food Colour. Position 2 small, flattened balls into the eye sockets and secure with edible glue.

10 Roll out the Black MMP, cut 2 ellipse shapes to fit in the centre of the eyes and secure with small dots of edible glue.

11 Cut whiskers from the fine silver wire and insert into the cheeks. Make sure you only insert them into the pads of paste under the outer covering: don't push them in too deeply as they must not come into contact with the cake.

important note

Remember to explain to the recipient of the cake that they must remove the wire whiskers and the paste they have penetrated before serving to be sure that the cake is safe to eat. If you are worried about using wires and would prefer to make the whiskers edible, you can make whiskers by extruding lengths of paste through the sugar shaper using the multi-hole disc. Straighten out the paste, cut to length and leave to dry. Once dry, insert these into the cheeks (make a hole for it to go through first using a cocktail stick: the paste will break if you try to insert it into the cake) then paint with edible silver paint.

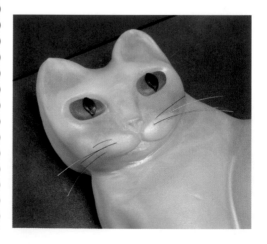

All templates are at 71%.

To enlarge templates to
actual size, increase them
by 141% (A4 to A3).

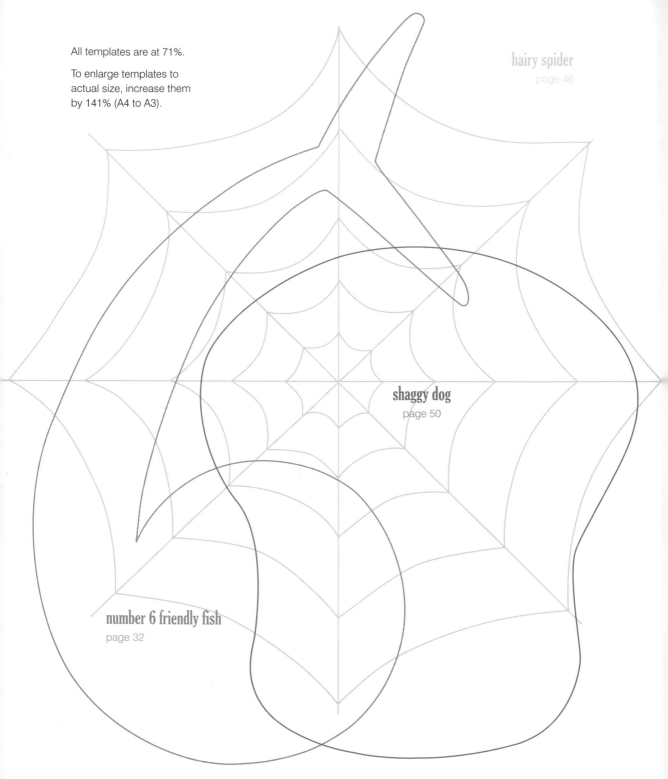

hairy spider
page 46

shaggy dog
page 50

number 6 friendly fish
page 32

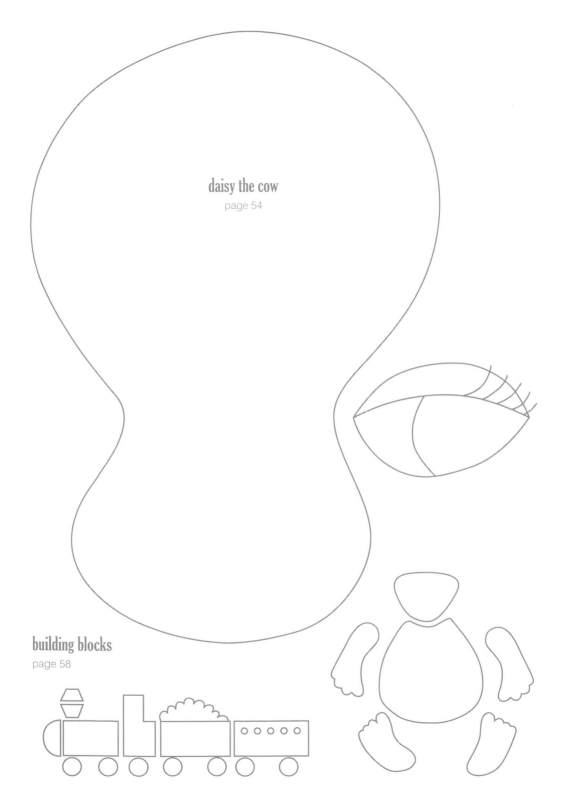

daisy the cow
page 54

building blocks
page 58

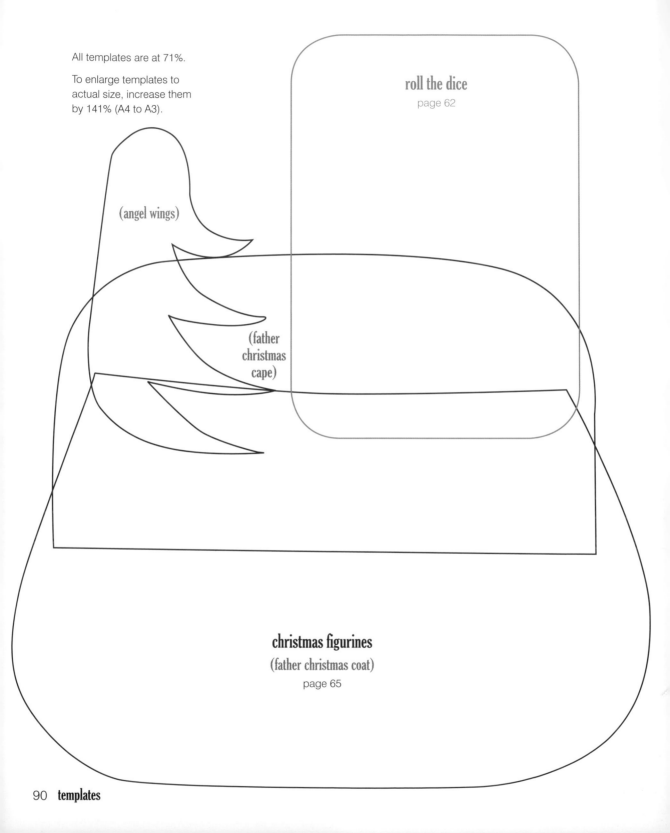

All templates are at 71%.

To enlarge templates to actual size, increase them by 141% (A4 to A3).

roll the dice
page 62

(angel wings)

(father christmas cape)

christmas figurines
(father christmas coat)
page 65

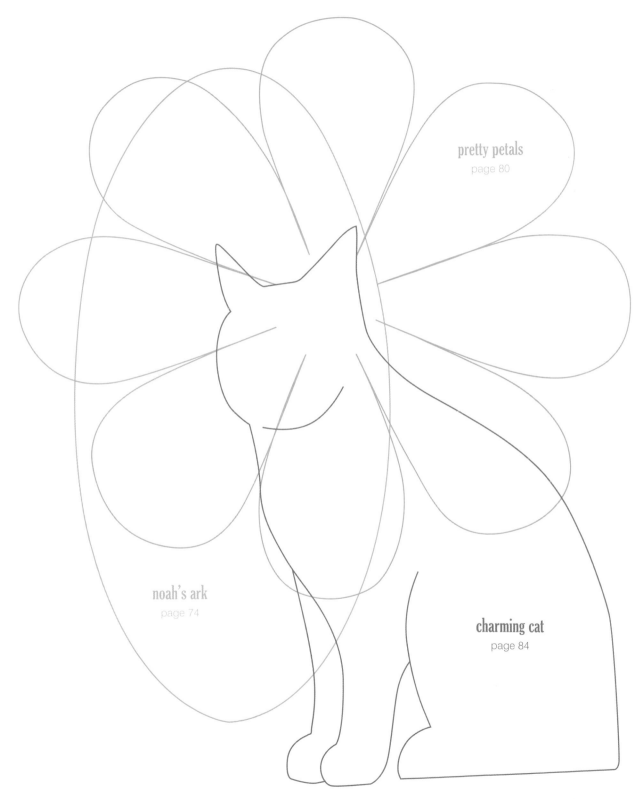

pretty petals
page 80

noah's ark
page 74

charming cat
page 84

suppliers

Squires Kitchen, UK

3 Waverley Lane
Farnham
Surrey
GU9 8BB
0845 61 71 810
+44 1252 260 260
www.squires-shop.com

Squires Kitchen International School

The Grange
Hones Yard
Farnham
Surrey
GU9 8BB
0845 61 71 812
+44 1252 260 262
www.squires-school.co.uk

Squires Kitchen, France

www.squires-shop.fr

Squires Kitchen, Spain

www.squires-shop.es

SK stockists

Jane Asher Party Cakes
London
020 7584 6177

Blue Ribbons
Surrey
020 8941 1591

Catering Complements
Kent
01892 513745

Lawsons Ltd.
Devon
01752 892543

The Sugarcraft Emporium
Worcestershire
01527 576703

Surbiton Art & Sugarcraft
Surrey
020 8391 4664

SK distributors

Guy Paul & Co. Ltd.
Buckinghamshire
www.guypaul.co.uk

Culpitt Ltd.
Northumberland
www.culpitt.com

Manufacturers

FMM Sugarcraft
Hertfordshire
www.fmmsugarcraft.com

Kit Box
North Somerset
www.kitbox.co.uk

Knightsbridge PME Ltd.
London
www.cakedecoration.co.uk

Lindy's Cakes
Buckinghamshire
www.lindyscakes.co.uk

Patchwork Cutters
Merseyside
www.patchworkcutters.com

Smeg UK Ltd.
www.smeguk.com
www.smegretro.co.uk
Italian appliance manufacturer
Smeg produces distinctive
domestic appliances combining
design, performance and quality.